Communal Violence in India

Communal Violence in India

P.R. Rajgopal

Under the Auspices of
Centre for Policy Research

UPPAL PUBLISHING HOUSE
NEW DELHI

UPPAL PUBLISHING HOUSE
3, Ansari Road, Daryaganj, New Delhi-110002

Fist Published, 1987

ISBN 81-85024-14-6

PRINTED IN INDIA
Published by B.S. Uppal, Uppal Publishing House
New Delhi-110002. Phototypeset by
Ess Bee Printers, B-17, Sector-8, NOIDA
Printed at Mehra Offset Press.

FOREWORD

Not very long ago, Shri L P Singh, one of our ablest public officials, brought to the notice of the nation the escalation of violence in India in recent years. The problem of violence is neither new to India nor to the other nations in the world. But some nations and civilizations appear to have tackled the issue better than some others.

What is the nature of violence in India ? Is it a major problematique of the India civilization as Prof Rajni Kothari states ? What are its sources ? And what are the practical policy options to deal with them ?

These are some of the central issues which we at the Centre for Policy Research debated at great length. We ultimately decided to request Shri P R Rajgopal one of the country's ablest police official to study the various dimension of the problem from a practical policy angle rather than from a wider academic point of view.

Shri Rajgopal examined violence in three essential dimensions in India. First the communal violence. Second violence arising out of socio-political change in India. And lastly organised crime and criminal justice.

We have decided to publish this triology as three separate studies though obviously they are highly interrelated.

The present study deals with the problem of communal violence as a practical official sees it. There is minimum of theory and a great deal of hard facts as they are available.

We do hope that the policy makers and the people in general will give a careful consideration to the various issues raised by Shri Rajgopal.

Centre for Policy Research
New Delhi-110 021.
March, 1987

V A Pai Panandiker
Director

Preface

This book is the first in a series of three studies. These studies are based on the research project "Violence in India" sponsored by the Centre for Policy Research, New Delhi. When the Director of the Centre for Policy Research, New Dèlhi, called upon me to undertake the study in July 1985, my idea at that point of time was to bring within the framework of one book the several aspects of violence that I intended to include in the study. Since then however, and as the study progressed, I realised that I would not be able to do adequate justice to the variety and the complexity of this multi-dimensional subject of violence unless I dealt with at least two or three of its important aspects in greater detail, in so far as they have direct and immediate relevance to the problems that are currently afflicting certain parts of the country. Hence I decided to split this study on violence in three separate parts. They are: 1) Communalism and communal violence; 2) Social change and violence; 3) Violence and Response—a study of the Criminal Justice System. This book is thus the first in the series. But for the support and financial help extended to me by the Centre for Policy Research, this study would not have been possible.

This book does not seek to project any theory on the subject of communalism. Much less does it seek to sit in judgement over the comparative merits and demerits of the religion. laws, customs and conventions governing the lives and lifestyles of the different communities. If therefore, in the course of this study, there is any observation which even vaguely gives any such impression, I can only say that no slight or hurt is intended to any community or religion on any of these accounts. This exercise is primarily an attempt at abstracting the different practical, as distinct from theroretical aspects that characterise and contribute to the phenomenon of communalism, and the complexity and variety of causes that give rise to communal violence. My only claim to write on a subject as delicate and sensitive as communalism is the fact of my having been a practising policeman for over thirty years. During this period, I have had several occasions not only of handling actual communal riots, but had also been charged with the responsibility of ensuring the peace of places which were communally highly sensitive. In the study that follows I have, therefore, drawn liberally from my own personal experiences in evaluating and assessing the several factors that contribute to making communalism a very important and, on that account regrettable fact of our national life. What appears in the pages that follow are more a projection of my perception of the communal problem as I see it and the several factors that contribute to creating it and giving it an unpardonable place in the socio-economic and political scheme of things. Even as the study progressed over the year, the communal virus has thrown deeper and more vicious roots which do not augur well for the country. It is my genuine hope and prayer that my prognosis of this disease, as it unfolds in the course of the study, will be proved wrong by the wisdom of our people and the statesmanship of our political leaders.

I am deeply grateful to Dr. V.A. Pai Panandiker, Director of the Centre for Policy Research, New Delhi, for giving me complete freedom to decide for myself the scope and the parameter of the study. His willing, generous and never failing help on several matters, both administrative and academic connected with the study, I acknowledge with utter gratefulness. I cannot thank adequately Shri. L.P. Singh for going through the contents of this, line by line, and making several meaningful suggestions by way of facts and ideas and above all, educating me on certain aspects of the national life to many of which he himself was a ringside observer if not an active participant. I am also grateful to several of my friends who had gone through the draft of this study at different stages and helped me with their ideas and suggestions. For the views expressed in the different contexts in the course of this study, I alone am responsible. The extensive secretarial help that Shri C. Jayaraman extended to me was invaluable.

P.R. RAJGOPAL

CONTENTS

I.

Introduction

"How inconceivably modest are human beings who bind themselves to only one religion! I have very many religions, and the one over-riding them is only forming throughout my life" (Elias Canetti, who won the Noble prize for literature in 1981). Is it not a pity that we should confine ourselves to only one religion when loyalty to and faith in more than one could have meant more by way of mutual peace and comaraderie? Apparently, there is a curse on the prevailing culture of consumerism which while rendering only a surplus of inanities as integral to it, rejects an additional one or more faith as an avoidable excess.

One area which has given rise to considerable violence during the last few years and which holds the potential for much more frightening violence than any other single cause is communalism. It is unfortunately true that we have a very long history of Hindu-Muslim communal violence, with a brief interval when it had distinctly abated in the years immediately following the gruesome partition riots. One cannot just wish away the revitalised components in the communal life of the country.

This study will limit itself to discussing only Hindu-Muslim communalism and the riots that are inevitably the wages of such communalism. This is, however, not to suggest that there are no other communal forces at play in the national scene. But Hindu-Muslim communalism has had a much longer history and deeper and more complex causes.

Until the eruption of the Punjab problem in its present militant form, Sikh communalism had not assumed the dimension that it is presently threatening to. It would not be quite correct to refer to the killing of the Sikhs in Delhi, Kanpur, Bokaro and a few other places that followed the assassination of the then Prime Minister in 1984, as communal riots. Even according to official figures, the number of people killed in Delhi alone during those five days following the assassination was around 3,000. The apparent justification for such mass killings was the fact that Smt. Indira Gandhi was shot by her own security guards who happened to be Sikhs. Wherever there were disturbances they were by and large a one-sided affair though there were a few Hindu casualties also. The total casualties reported from Uttar Pradesh were 174 including 30 bodies which were recovered from trains. Out of a total recovery of property valued at Rs. 3.7 crores in Uttar Pradesh, Kanpur alone accounted for Rs. 2.64 crores. In Bihar, 107 people in all were killed. Bokaro in Bihar reported 75 deaths. The trouble in Bokaro was attributed to rivalry between Sikh and non-Sikh contractors on the one hand, and non-Sikh businessmen who had been depending on loans from the Sikhs. The debtors apparently wanted to shake themselves free of the burden of repayment. They utilised the occasion for the purpose. One hopes that communal riot as we know it between Hindus and Muslims will not become yet another endemic feature between Hindus and Sikhs also. This hope has been to an extent dimmed by the events in the Punjab in the first eight months of 1986.

Operation Blue Star, launched by the Army in the Golden Temple at Amritsar, had roused the ire of the Sikh population generally all over the country against the government. The assassination of Mrs. Indira Gandhi, which can be said to be a sequel to it, followed by the killing of the Sikhs in such large numbers in certain places in the country, has brought about a degree of communal animosity in relations between sections of Hindus and Sikhs in the Punjab. The relations between these two communities have suffered a further setback because of the assassination of the ex-Chief of the Army Staff, Gen. A.S. Vaidya at Pune on 10th August, 1986.

Even so, compared to Hindu-Muslim conflicts there is a qualitative difference, at least as of now, in the Hindu-Sikh communal conflict that has surfaced in the first eight months of 1986. Both communities have shown considerable restraint, and the minority population of Hindus in the rural areas and the Sikhs in some of the urban areas of Punjab continue to live in peace and amity under the most difficult conditions. This is inspite of the provocations of a handful of terrorist groups and a section of extremists among the Sikhs, and a section of Hindus who are the followers of the Shiv Sena. The points of contact and similarity in the ways of life of the two communities are so many that communal feelings between them, one hopes, will not reach the point of becoming chronic as it unfortunately has become between Hindus and Muslims. This assumption is based on the fact of the relationship that exists between the two communities, which extends to what is termed as "Beti-Roti" relationship i.e. a relationship which permits inter-marriages and partaking of food.

The relationship between Christians and Hindus has generally been cordial and harmonious, though occasionally there have been some tensions caused by conversion in tribal areas.

This study is in three parts. The first part, while identifying the factors which contribute to communalism, has also dealt briefly with communal politics in the context of Kerala. Muslim communalism arising out of the issue of Muslim Personal Law and the nature and level of Muslim education have been discussed in some detail. The reason for treating the subject of Muslim Personal Law at such length is that it is a potential cause of communal violence. Muslim education has been discussed in detail in the context of the charge that Muslims are being discriminated against, in the sphere of employment.

The second part deals briefly with some of the factors which have been responsible for riots at certain places in Bihar, Uttar Pradesh, Gujarat, Maharashtra and Karnataka.

An attempt has been made to assemble the factors responsible for creating the volatile conditions and the atmosphere of communal sensitivity in which even the flimsiest of incidents sparks off a communal carnage. An effort has also been made to draw a few important lessons from the handling of the different riots that had taken place in the recent past. The extent to which the lessons so drawn are applied on the ground will decide whether or not similar situations arising in future can be handled with much less loss of life and property, and with greater speed and efficiency. The point that is being sought to be driven home is that, even if we cannot completely eliminate communal riots, it is possible to take steps in advance which can distinctly reduce the devastation and cruelty and with it the trail of agony and bitterness that are left behind by these senseless riots.

The third part attempts to spell out the implications of secularism. The study concludes with a discussion on those aspects in the relationship between the communities which have kept them together and which in fact are our islands of hope. Our only chance of survival as a democratic and secular nation is by enlarging and expanding the nature and scope of these fruitful and goodwill generating relationships.

It is difficult to write on a subject like communalism and communal violence without drawing fire from communalists of whatever hue, for views held or opinions expressed, however honestly and objectively. But to muffle or mute the message for that reason will be nothing less than an exercise in evasion if not in downright intellectual dishonesty. This exercise has been undertaken with a view to assess the extent and volume of communalism in the body politic. It is not my intention to apportion blame or responsibility to any of the communities. If however, facts add up in favour of or against one or the other community at different times, it only means that communalism, unlike consumer durables, does not lend itself to weighing in a balance; nor is it prudent or desirable to approach this cancerous subject on the basis of "we" or "they". The point that is being sought to be established is that communalism even as it prevails currently, be it of the Hindu or of the Muslim variety, has gone into the lethal stage in terms of dosage. Once the threshold is crossed, it matters little whether Hindu communalism is more blatant than Muslim communalism or the reverse. Hindu and Muslim communalism exist in each other's perception, be it real or imaginary and are both equally toxic. When the two conflict with each other, they consume cruelly all that comes their way, leaving neither victor nor vanquished behind, but a nation wounded mortally. I have handled riots and I have been a witness to the decimation that communal carnage can cause. Every successive communal riot deals a body blow not so much to the Hindus or the Muslims, but to the India of our hopes and dreams. Let it be realised that with every riot the status and stature of India shrinks—maybe even irretrievably. As and when, therefore, the communal bell tolls, let it be understood that it tolls for thee, for every Indian. If therefore, this paper is able to identify some of the factors which contribute to communalism, and to highlight our unforgivable failure to combat it as a nation, the exercise would have vindicated itself.

II.

Incidence of Riots

The incidence of communal riots between Hindus and Muslims has increased over the years and this trend shows no signs of being reversed. This unfortunate fact has to be squarely faced. In terms of statistics, the following table is fairly eloquent:

Table I
Number of Communal Incidents and Persons Killed and Injured in these Incidents During 1954 to 1985

Sl. No.	Year	No. of incidents	Persons killed	Persons injured
1.	1954	84	34	512
2.	1955	75	24	457
3.	1956	82	35	575
4.	1957	58	12	316
5.	1958	40	7	369
6.	1959	42	41	1344
7.	1960	26	14	262
8.	1961	92	108	593
9.	1962	60	43	348
10.	1963	61	26	489
11.	1964	1070	1919	2053
12.	1965	173	34	758

Sl. No.	Year	No. of incidents	Persons killed	Persons injured
13.	1966	144	45	467
14.	1967	198	251	880
15.	1968	346	133	1309
16.	1969	519	673	2702
17.	1970	521	298	1607
18.	1971	321	103	1263
19.	1972	240	69	1056
20.	1973	242	72	1318
21.	1974	248	87	1123
22.	1975	205	33	890
23.	1976	169	39	794
24.	1977	188	36	1122
25.	1978	230	110	1853
26.	1979	304	261	2379
27.	1980	421	372	2691
28.	1981	319	196	2613
29.	1982	470	238	3025
30.	1983	500	1143	3652
31.	1984	476	445	4836
32.	1985	525	328	3665

The figures quoted are from official sources. The official figures of casualties tend to be lower than the actual figures. Even so, if one were to go only by the official figures, the trend in terms of the number of incidents is sufficiently disturbing and the intensity of the problem as borne out by the number of dead and injured is alarmingly large for us to feel concerned about the current state of communal affairs in the country. Every communal riot, apart from being a reflection of the health of the society that we live in, also aggravates the differences between the communities to a point when over a period of time it may make reconciliation and peaceful co-existence between the communities more and more difficult.

While the increase in the incidence of communal riots is bad enough, what makes it worse is the spread that this virus has acquired over the years. According to the study conducted by Gopal Krishna(I), in 1961 there were 61 districts in the country which had experienced communal trouble in that year. By 1970, the number of districts afflicted by the virus had spread to 216, representing 70 per cent of the basic administrative units. Taking the 1971 town classification, 10.77 per cent of all the towns in the country had experienced communal violence. Making a statement in the Parliament on 24th July 1986 on the communal situation in the country, the Home Minister stated that 88 districts had been identified as hypersensitive and 98 as sensitive districts from the communal point of view.

The states particularly affected are: Assam, West Bengal, Bihar, Uttar Pradesh, Gujarat, Madhya Pradesh, Maharashtra, Karnataka, Kerala and Andhra Pradesh. Reckoned in terms of serious communal incidents, in 1982 there were 17 major incidents which accounted for the death of 121 persons and injuries to 520; in 1983, if the Assam incidents are excluded, there were 9 serious incidents resulting in the death of 89 persons, with 910 injured. About 2300 persons were reported to have lost their lives in Assam in 1983 which included also the killings at Nelle. The Nelle carnage was one of the worst after the partition riots. In 1984 there were 17 serious incidents which accounted for 344 perons killed and 2300 injured. The official estimates of the loss of property in commounal riots were Rs. 18 lakhs in 1981, Rs. 3.62 crores in 1982, Rs. 1.34 crores in 1983 and a staggering Rs. 9.9 crores in 1984.

Of the total of 525 incidents in 1985, 96 were in Gujarat, 65 in Bihar, 61 in West Bengal, 51 in Maharashtra, 48 in Karnataka, 45 in Andhra Pradesh, 41 in Uttar Pradesh, 31 in Madhya Pradesh, 24 in Rajasthan, 21 in Kerala, 14 in Tamil Nadu, 10 in Orissa, 8 in Jammu and Kashmir, 7 in Assam and 3 in Delhi. The spread of the virus is worth noting; it has spread to states which had been free from this in the past.

According to an analysis of the incidents that took place in 1982, of the 470 incidents, 124 were due to religious causes such as playing of music before mosques or taking out religious processions on unapproved routes; 45 were due to incidents of improper behaviour towards women; 43 due to land disputes; 9 due to elections, and 249 due to miscellaneous causes.

According to an analysis of the incidents of 1985, in 132 of the riots the provocation was due to religous causes, 47 riots were due to misbehaviour towards women, 261 due to miscellaneous causes, 45 due to land disputes and 40 were concerned with the anti-reservation agitation. The political parties contributed as usual to communal violence during the general elections of 1984 and 1985, apparently because of the advantage that they expected to derive therefrom by the polarisation of the electorate on communal lines. Electioneering led to major communal violence in Uttar Pradesh, Bihar, Karnataka and Gujarat.

As a general proposition, communal riots occur in places where neither of the communities has a preponderance in number. More riots occur in districts which have a Muslim population varying between 15 per cent and 59.3 per cent. The population of Hindus and Muslims in the important cities and towns which have been the scenes of serious communal riots is given in table-2 :

Table 2
Population percentage in some of the communally prone cities

	Hindus	Muslims
Hyderabad	37.5%	59.3%
Bhiwandi	41.5%	52.4%
Kalyan	73.1%	17.9%
Meerut	55.4%	40.9%
Moradabad	51.2%	47.4%
Aligarh	63.7%	34.4%
Nalanda (Biharsharif)	61.0%	38.7%

In the past, communal riots were largely an urban phenomenon. But now the virus has spread to the rural areas also. According to an official estimate, the rural areas reported 46 per cent of the communal incidents in 1985.

III

Factors Contributing to Communalism

There are several factors which contribute to the generation and aggravation of communalism among religious groups. An attempt has been made to identify a few of the more important among these. Each of these factors, individually and collectively, contributes to creating the communal atmosphere in which even the mildest of provocations erupts into irrational violence. Both Hindu and Muslim groups contribute to this communally combustible situation, and to that extent both the communities are equally responsible. Above all, how the members of the respective communities perceive each other's conduct at the street level is what determines the eruption and the scale of communal violence. Thus considered, there is not much scope for formulating what in effect is an irrational and impulsive communal aggressiveness within the confines of a neat sociological theory.

It would be naive to suggest that there is any single cause or a simple solution to this festering problem between Hindus and Muslims, which has visibly increased over the years. Even so, in Independent India we have not made any comprehensive study of the problem in all its various complexities and ramifications. It would appear that we are living from riot to riot, using the intervening period not so much in understanding the basic causes which contributed to the earlier ones, but without deliberate intent, in effect actually contributing to and promoting further the causes which make future riots possible. We are unintentionally making every succeeding riot easier to provoke and more devastating and destructive in result than the preceding ones.

The riots, any riot for that matter, are used as occasions for giving expression to the pent up anger that individuals and groups have against the system as a whole, though the immediate targets are the visible symbols of authority and the system. The prime cause for this anger is lack of work, lack of decent housing and other civic amenities, and the lack of hope that things would improve in the near future. It is easy to understand why they burn cars and loot shops. For at least a little while the rioter is someone. He and the fellow rioters have an identity. The police confront them and the leaders appeal to them for peace. For once, on such occasions, they get the satisfaction of being noticed as individuals in their own right. In the case of communal riot however, every riot sharpens the separate indentity of the communal groups and particularly the identity of the minority groups. The process by itself, whether it is intended or not, promotes the role of communal leadership and gives it an extra dimension. Thus over a period of time, communal leadership develops a vested interest in communal riots, as with every successive riot the demands and reliance on the communal leaders increase. In the context of the prevailing anger and hatred, the leader who speaks increasingly in favour of or against the other group, grows in stature and importance in the eyes of the people of his group. Unscrupulous communal leaders thereafter exploit this leadership for narrow sectarian ends regardless of the interests of the society as a whole. The accent today is on the separateness of the religious groups rather than on the factors integrating them together as one people of the country. Whether one likes to face it or not, this is a fact of the national scene which one cannot either wish away or ignore. As long as this trend persists, we will have to live with the monster of communalism which will fatten and grow on communal bloodshed.

As in the case of a fire, the immediate cause of a communal riot by itself does not explain the entire run of circumstances which may have contributed to its eventual outbreak. The fact of such human combustibility has to be viewed and understood in the context of the several factors which make the people of the area communally sensitive to the slightest catalyst which may appear on the scene. But treating the catalyst as the main cause would be to misunderstand the enitire psychology of the rioters and the real causes behind the riots. Every riot has to be treated as an event in search of a meaning and significance. It is exactly because we look at each of the riots in isolation and are not prepared to go beyond the periphery of each one of them that we fail to understand the meaning and the message that they seek to convey. In the process we fail to identity the causes precisely, and to apply the correctives which alone can prevent riots from becoming endemic.

Regardless of what is or what is not contained in our Constitution, when two Gods lay claim to the same piece of land and promote a fight between their respective followers in which several innocnet persons lose their lives, the least that we can say of ourselves is that we are far, far behind the development of secular consciousness. Let us accept this fact in all honesty, instead of bandying about the words secular and secularism which mean many things to many people and contrary things to conflicting communities.

Communalism as an ideology is the ultimate source of all communal riots. The beneficiaries of this ideology are also its promoters who seek to achieve certain personal or group interests by articulating the secular needs of the community on communal lines. When demands raised on communal lines are even considered, let alone accepted by the government, it is not so much the community which benefits but the few communalists who use the occasion to build up their image in the community.

(a) Religious Revival and Hindu and Muslim Perceptions about each other

There is a general religous revival among the different communities in our country. This by itself is not bad. The new found faith in religion by the communities has however been giving rise to several problems. One of these is that the fervour for one's religion is often measured by fanatics against the ferocity that they display against the other religion. They give the impression that they are not so much imbued with the belief in the tenets of their own religion as by the fanaticism and the muscle power that they display in safeguarding what they think are the legitimate interests of the respective Gods. They would almost have us believe that shorn of the muscle power of the followers, the Gods are powerless and helpless on their own. When our faith in providence is reduced to such absurd and meaningless trials of strength, religion becomes a facade and an alibi for short-term personal or political mileage. What these fanatical protagonists of the respective religions do not understnad or do not want to understand is that they cannot save their religion by such methods. What is more, religions which can be saved only by such violent methods do not deserve to be saved.

When Emerson said, "Once we had wooden chalices and golden priests; now we have golden chalices and wooden priests", he was saying something which is very fundamental to the change that has come about in the relationship that men have to their religious institutions. There was a newspaper report to the effect that the temple at Ayodhya is likely to be rebuilt at a cost of Rs. 25 crores. Vast sums of money are being spent on renovating and restructuring mosques. If the current manifestations of what passes for religous faith is any guide, we seem to be for ever building bigger and bigger temples and mosques and killing the creed. If the particular religion that people profess does not create in them the spirit of resolving the differences when possible and rising above them where necessary, it only means that the people concerned are interested in the form rather than the substance of religion.

For such people secularism is an anathema. They do not understand even the implications of the concept. They are far, far removed from practising it.

The tone and tenor of the articles written by Hindu and Muslim communalists and the beliefs that they nurse about the other community have been brought out by the Centre for Rural Research and Industrial Development, Chandigarh, which did a study of the Bhiwandi riots of 1984 and the Pune riots of 1982. The following extracts are reproduced from the study (2).

"In Bhiwandi and Pune cities the generally prevailing impression about the Muslims among the Hindus are:

Islam is devouring Hinduism; Islam is a militant religion. It preaches brutality. Muslims believe in one God and one Book and are more organized. They are orthodox and fanatical. Muslims continue to be aliens and they do not adhere to the Indian Civil Code. If you visit a Muslim family, you will find one Muslim married to at least four women and each one of these women bears many children. Muslims have no work other than reproduction. Since Muslims do not follow the Indian Civil Code, they will have to pay the penalty of leaving India. Muslims are immoral. Muslims want to numerically out-number Hindus through conversion and the violation of the small family norms so as to establish another Pakistan in India.

Similarly, impressions which are prevalent among sections of the Muslim groups about Hindus in Bhiwandi and Pune are as follows:

> Except Islam, all religions are adulterated. Superstition is the nick name of Hinduism. Hindus are stingy and money-minded. Hindus can mortgage their wives and daughters for money. Hindus charge interest on money. They loan money on extraordinary interest rates whereas interest is prohibited in Islam. While Muslims

impart moral teachings to children, Hindus teach their young ones methods of spinning money.

"Muslim India" is a monthly journal of reference, research and documentation. A glance at some of the issues of "Muslim India" leaves one with the impression that it is prone to feeding Muslim communalism. This is done in the following manner.:—

Highlighting the under-representation of Muslims in jobs and services in one of its issues, the said journal gives elaborate statistics on Muslim representation in different classes of functionaries in High Courts. A High Court judge is treated as a representative of the whole Muslim religious group and his apointment is shown to be a service to the religous group to which he belongs.... political and other communal groups use this data by feeding to the perception of the people that benefits are distributed on communal basis. Such propaganda also identifies the causes of deprivation falsely... Communal categories are spared while quoting figures on Institutions which are commonly believed to have been monopolised by different religous groups. For example, the data on Aligarh Muslim University is prsented without identifying the strength of students, teachers, ete. on religious group lines. The Hindu communalists generally interpret this as an attempt by Muslim communalists to hide the gradual alienation of non-Muslims from the University. They further accuse the journal of dishonesty by always beating its breast on missed opportunities, but concealing its grin on the availed ones."

'Sobat', a Marathi weekly, in its issue dated May 6, 1984 under a blatantly communal title "Musulmans cannot live in Hindustan" published the following:

"The very concept of a nation is opposed to Koran. Therefore, if they are not having any feeling of affection for this country, it is Koran. Character of Koran Shariat, i.e. Islamic system of governance is opposed to our Constitution and Law. If we have faith in our Constitution, we will have to ban Koran and Islamic system of governance."

Some of the Kannada and Marathi writings which had appeared at Belgaum in Karnataka on the eve of the 1984 riot would have put to shame the worst communalists. Yet nothing much was done by the authorities to stop this scurrilous anti-Muslim propaganda. Hindu and Muslim communalism feed on and fuel each other. With such supreme indifference to rank communalism displayed unhindered, why should we be surprised if this poison erupts periodically into vicious communal violence?

The reports of commissions on communal riots devote considerable time and space to describing the immediate causes which had provoked the riots. What is important is that in an atmosphere which is charged with communal passion, the immediate cause which ignites communal feelings in individuals can be even the flimsiest one. To emphasize that to the exclusion of the breeding and imbibing of the communal ideology in day to day politics and conduct, all of which over a period of time divide the communities into distinct groups, who react to even the most trivial thing such as a quarrel between two children belonging to two different communities in a communal manner, is to mistake the tree for the forest. For communal leaders the number of men of the respective communities who get killed and whose houses get looted or burnt are merely means to the furtherance of their own vested interests. These poor victims are fed on the diet of communalism day in and day out, and in their genuine but blind faith in their religion they willingly become mere pawns in the games that the communal vested interests play. The individuals who get killed in communal riots or who suffer damages can be compared to the bullets which one who handles a firearm uses to achieve a particular objective. He uses the bullets as expendable items towards the furtherance of his cause. He does not feel sorry for them. He does not have second thoughts for the spent bullets. The story is the same with the communalists who use these poor people living in congested localities huddled together and without even the basic civic amentities, and who perpetually are in a state of discomfort, anger and tension, as just bullets to serve their diabolical communal design. If therefore, we are to make a dent into communalism, this will have to begin with the politicians, the intellectuals and the businessmen who will have to pursue their respective professions on non-communal lines: rather a tall order, more easily given than acted upon. Communalism was exploited in the pre-partition days by leaders for a share of power at the centre, which eventually culminated in the partition of the country. In Independent India, ironically enough, communalism has been exploited by the communalists for secular ends. The passions of the mass of the population who are illiterate and ignorant are played upon by the minority community leaders by creating in them a sense of insecurity, discrimination, persecution and above all a sense of loss of identity, should they not combine to stand up against the common enemy which is projected as Hindu chauvinism. As against this, the Hindu communalists and organisations such as Vishwa Hindu Parishad (V.H.P.) have been propagating through their writings and speeches that the Muslims are conspiring to upset the demographic composition of the Indian population by not falling in line with the state sponsored Family Planning Programme to limit the number of children, and also through conversion. The mass conversion of Harijans to Islam in Meenakshipuram among other places in Tamil Nadu is cited as evidence.

The increase in population of the Muslims may be due to whatever reason. The V.H.P. cite the Census figures in support of their stand. The net result is the grist that all these add to the communal mill.

Table 3

Percentage increase of Population of Hindus and Muslims in the three Census of 1961, 1971 and 1981

	In 1961 over 1951			In 1971 over 1961			In 1981 over 1971		
	A.C.	Hindus	Muslims	A.C.	Hindu	Muslims	A.C.	Hindu	Muslims
All India	21.64	20.74	32.54	24.80	23.71	30.85	24.74*	24.19*	30.59*
Bihar	19.76	18.96	32.29	21.30	19.54	31.26	24.06	23.34	30.03
Kerala	24.76	23.23	27.50	26.29	23.35	37.49	19.24	16.70	29.96
Uttar Pradesh	16.66	16.13	19.48	19.79	18.52	26.77	25.49	24.82	29.11
West Bengal	32.80	32.63	36.48	26.87	25.75	29.76	23.17	21.37	29.55

Note :

A.C. - All communities

* - Excluding Assam

Source : 1) For figures 1961 over 1951 : Statistical Abstract India (1970) (Page : 32 Page : 40)

2) Census of India 1971; Series 1-India Paper-2 of 1972 Religion

3) Census of India 1981; Paper 4 of 1984 (Series-1 India)

The V.H.P. has been the moving spirit behind the agitation to get the disputed temple at Ayodhya opened. How an ostensibly religious demand is given a communal slant for political purposes is evident from the declaration made by the V.H.P. as far back as October, 1984 that the Hindus exercising their franchise in the then impending general elections was contingent on the Ayodhya temple being reopened for worship. One of the pamphlets issued by the V.H.P. carried the observation that "lack of collective thinking for the protection of Hindu interests... is the main cause of the miserable and disgraceful condition of the Hindu society.... Each individual of Hindu Samaj.... should cast his vote in the forthcoming election for a candidate, irrespective of his party affiliations, who gives an undertaking to support the 5 points enumerated. One of these points was: "to pass an act, to return to Hindu Samaj the original places of Ram Janma Bhumi, Shri Krishna Jamma Bhumi and Kashi Vishwanath temple"(3).

It needs to be realised that Hindu communal organisations like the V.H.P. and the Hindu Mahasabha which did not have much political following until recently, are now beginning to have a larger say in the electoral politics of the country in some states. Though their impact is only marginal, they do fuel the communal feelings which others take advantage of during the elections. They influence the voting pattern though they themselves do not have electoral successes in the absence of any electoral organisation. There is nothing to choose between Hindu and Muslim communalism.

The events that followed the unlocking of the Ayodhya temple/Babari mosque on February Ist, 1986 are now a part of history. The Pakistani shadow on Indian communal politics was evident when Pakistan's Interior Minister Noorani made a statement in the Pak National Assembly that Pakistan would not remain indifferent to the fate of their co-religionists in India. This was followed by an attack on the Hindu temples and the few Hindus in Karachi, which was a sequel to the communal riots in Delhi and other places in India. To pretend that such policy pronouncements by Pakistani leaders do not have an impact on the communal situation in our country is not to understand what Pakistan stands for and seeks to achieve in the subcontinent. This trend is likely to persist because of the historical background arising out of the partition of India. Exploiting the communal happenings in India has been an integral part of the geopolitics of Pakistan. Pakistan stands to gain considerable diplomatic mileage by fuelling communal politics in India, as with every communal riot, India's stock with Middle East and other Islamic countries suffers a diplomatic setback. Considering the advantages Pakistan stands to gain in this regard, it should be reasonable to suspect that Pakistan would also have a vested interest in promoting it. One tends to agree with the observations of the Minority commission, which is obviously pointing to Pakistan in the extract quoted below.

The Minority Commission in its Fourth Annual Report for the period 01-01-1981 to 31-03-1982 observed: "We cannot overlook the fact that there are foreign as well as internal elements likely to be interested in creating disorder and making out that there is genocide and maltreatment of minorities in India. There are some political parties also interested in showing that governments in power are unable to preserve law and order to safeguard the interests of the minorities. The existence of unscrupulous schemers abroad and in our country who think on these lines rather than on the welfare of minorities in India or of the whole country should not surprise anybody."

On the morning of 15th August, 1985 Kashmir Valley woke up to pro-Pak and anti-India slogans: "Long live Pakistan. Indian dogs go back". Within hours, Pakistani flags were hoisted on top of the electric poles. India' Independence Day was observed as a Black Day by some anti-national elements. Ghulam Nabi Khayal writing under the title: 'Unrest in the Valley' (4) observed : "On every Friday from pulpits of 20,000 odd mosques and shrines over the Valley, Muslim priests raise their hands and pray loudly from the Koran: "Fa-Ansura Alal Quamil Kaafireen (2:286) (give us victory over the non-believers, the Kafirs) and millions of faithfuls say 'Amen' in thunderous supplication. The non-believers i.e. the Kafirs for many Kashmiri Muslims are none other than the Hindus of India."

In another instance, the Jamma & Kashmir government claimed to have arrested 500 persons stated to be anti-national elements in different parts of the state on the eve of Republic Day in 1986. Some of them had been planning to hoist the Pakistan flag, according to the police. All such activities, apparently inspired by the fundamentalists among the Muslims, are not likely to be ignored and go without being reacted to by the bigoted among the Hindus in other parts of the country.

One of the features of Kashmir politics in recent times has been the rise of a type of leadership in Kashmir which sees nothing wrong in openly advocating Islamic fundamentalism in the affairs of the state. The national family planning programme is opposed openly and the Muslims are advised not to follow the programme. One of the leaders even offers to shelter the wards of the poor Muslim families who are unable to look after their children.

The Kashmir Pradesh Congress-I President Mufti Mohd. Syed, addressing a series of public meetings at several places in the Kashmir Valley in the third week of April, 1986, is reported to have said that the fundamentalists and anti-social elements were busy conducting a "hate campaign against nationalists" and forging unity with the secessionists in the state. He is reported to have urged that unless the state administration checks them with an iron hand, the situation will continue to be disturbing(5).

For a section of the population in Jammu and Kashmir, Kashmir continues to be a disputed issue. This attitude can be a cause of giving an edge to Hindu-Muslim communal discord in other parts of the country. The threat by a section of Kashmiri Muslims to launch a 'Jehad' for the liberation of Kashmir from India is not likely to be viewed with equanimity by the rest of the country.

In the Kashmir Valley, there have been in the last couple of years cases of explosion and arson affecting road communication. These have been attributed to pro-Pak elements. According to reliable sources, as against 13 bomb explosions and 12 arson cases during 1984, the number of such incidents went up to 20 and 34 respectively during 1985.

The communalists and the extremists among the Sikhs add an extra dimension to the communal problem in Jammu and Kashmir. In view of the support that Pakistan has been extending to both the Sikh extremists and the pro-Pak anti-national elements among the Muslims in Jammu and Kashmir, it is to be expected that the communal situation in Jammu and Kashmir will get more heated. This is likely to aggravate the communal situation in the other parts of the country. That the Sikh extremists and the pro-Pak and secessionist elements in Jammu and Kashmir have a programme of subversion and sabotage should be evident from the abortive effort made jointly by the Sikh extremists and the pro-Pak anti-national Muslim elements in Jammu and Kashmir to hijack an Indian Airlines plane from Jammu to Pakistan in September, 1985. This operation was to coincide with the date of the elections in Punjab. Fortunately, the attempt was foiled because of the vigilance of the security forces.

Frank Camper who runs a private paramilitary training camp in Alabama, United States, in the course of an article in the American magazine Penthouse in March, 1986 quoted an unidentified Sikh as telling him that some of the Sikh extremists who had undergone training in his school had told him that both China and Pakistan have been aiding the extremist Sikh cause, providing money, weapons as well as safe areas inside their own respective borders for training and hiding(6).

The communal riot that rocked Jammu and Kashmir in February-March, 1986, which was a sequel to the Ayodhya Temple/Babari Mosque issue, and which brought down in the process the Shah Ministry, is also a pointer to the potential the communal virus has in creating turmoil in the country.

An additional element which is likely to intensify communal feeling is the belief that is gaining ground both among the Sikh extremists and the pro-Pak elements in Jammu and Kashmir, that should Khalistan come into being, the secession of the Kashmir Valley from India may be facilitated. The communalism that had been raging in Jammu and Kashmir as also in the rest of the country has to be viewed not as a passing phenomenon between the two communities but as an integral component of the geo-politics of Pakistan and the other foreign powers who may be interested in destabilising the country.

Hindu communalists have also been organising themselves under an organisation called Shiv Sena in the Jammu region, where during 1985 they clashed with Sikh extemists several times. The clashes have however remained largely localised.

b) Communal Politics

Muslims in India as a community had suffered the trauma of the partition of the country. They started emerging out of this state from the sixties and have become once again a self-confident and asseritve group wanting to take their legitimate place in the national scheme of things, while retaining their distinct identity. There is also the emergence of a middle class among the Muslims which was almost non-existent immediately following the Partition, as most of the middle class Muslims from several states had migrated to Pakistan, leaving behind Muslims who were economically and educationally backward, and also a few who were part of the professional elite. The new middle class among the Muslims that has come up has done so on the basis of its own strenuous efforts and inspite of the several factors which may have impeded their progress.

The socio-economic changes in the country being brought about through the various planned programmes have benefitted the different communities in varying degrees. The Muslims as a community have also gained from several of these programmes. The boom in the economy of the Arab countries in the Middle East has been a blessing to thousands of Indian job seekers belonging to all the communities in India. The youth and the entrepreneurs among the Muslims have also captitalised on this boom. This accounts for a distinct spurt in the economic affluence of Muslims in certain parts of the country. Reports from Moradabad and Varanasi in Uttar Pradesh and Mallapuram, Kasargode and Calicut districts of Kerala, and other places in the country point to the fact of the Muslims making considerable investments in real estate. Large and affluent Muslim townships have sprung up particularly in Uttar Pradesh and Kerala during the last couple of decades. All these are postive trends which should in due course countribute, one expects, to the development of a healthy relationship between the communities. Because of the active and the avowed interest that the government has taken to promote the concept of reservation, regrettably a belief has come into being that the government would respond only if demands are projected on the basis of a group identity such as caste or community. The result has been that the communities have also tended to consolidate themselves in an effort to project their identity to demand their share of the scarce economic resources, and educational and job opportunities.

Politics in general is a process of conflict resolution. In trying to resolve this conflict each of the participating and contending groups and communities seeks to gain terms as advantageous and favourable to it as possible. The democratic constitution which we have given ourselves has unfortunately tended to become a very fertile breeding ground for the manipulative politics of the communities and the groups, and this has not been without its injurious impact on the general political health of the country. Since democracy in its ultimate form is a function of numbers and a game of pressure groups, the different caste and community groups seek to promote the inerests of their respective communities by exercising the political leverage that they have to the maximum extent possible. The effort therefore of each of the groups is to acquire as much political power as possible and with it the political leverage as a means to further enhance community or caste interests. The growth of communalism therefore should be seen as a means to achieve as much political power as possible, since the leverage which political power confers is what the communal leaders think ultimately matters in the dispensation that the community stands to get from the centres of power. Nowhere is this proposition demonstrated in such clear and unmistakeable terms as in Kerala today. This will be dealt with in detail later.

It is indeed unfortunate that in the first place a belief should at all have grown that an individual or a group or a communtiy can get justice only by organising themselves into identifiable groups and communities. This belief having been created for whatever reasons in the context of our socio-economic inheritance, it tends to get perpetuated and strengthened by the successive concessions that some of these groups and communities have received in response to demands made on communal lines. Every such concession gives a fresh lease of hope and sustenance to communalism, while at the same time eroding the roots of secularism and integration. In an atmosphere polluted by communalism anthing done in the national life with regard to administrative measures, education, socio-economic change, trade and commerce, is seen by the individuals of the communities concerned who cannot cash in on any of these for their personal benefits as an act of discrimination by the government against the community as a whole. Such individuals, as also the communities as a whole, are impervious or even callous to the fact that for every individual of the community who has been disappointed and frustrated there are several others similarly disappointed in the other communities. Disappointment and frustration of individuals and groups is inevitable in any developing country and more so in a country like India with its exploding population, scarce resources and limited opportunities. When what in fact is a socio-economic disability or inadequacy is sought to be attributed to communal motivations and discriminations, we have the different communities of the country set on a collision course. In an atmosphere which stands thus vitiated on communal lines one would have expected the political parties of the country to refrain from doing anything which would only feed and strengthen the communal virus. Instead if the political parties in their anxiety to come to or stay in power communalise the game to a pitch which would neutralize or even dilute the several factors which have contributed to secularising and integrating the country as a whole, it would be a great tragedy.

c) Communal Politics of Kerala : A warning

Considered in this context the present state of affairs in Kerala has an increasing relevance to the communal scenario in the rest of the country. I have therefore discussed the communal politics of Kerala in some detail in the hope that political parties in other parts of the country will look upon the politics of Kerala not as an example to be followed but as an unmistakeable warning about the dangers that lie ahead if the politics of the country is reduced to an equation of political strength with the vigour of communal organisation. Kerala presents a classic illustration of how politics when played with only short term interests in view can contribute substantially to communalism.

Kerala is distinctly different in certain aspects from the rest of the country. It has the highest density of population. The human settlements in the state are stretched from end to end in one vast and continuous urban like set up. The composition of the population is also different from the rest of the country. According to the 1981 Census, the religious composition of the population is as follows:

Table 4
Percentage of population according to Community

Religions	India* %	Kerala %
Hindus	82.64	58.16
Muslims	11.35	21.25
Christians	2.43	20.56
Others	3.58	0.03

Note: * Excludes Assam

The minority communities in the State while forming substantial groups are also the dominant communities in certain districts. The size and the distribution of the minority population have had distinct socio-economic and political implications. The proportion of the educated in Kerala is 60%, which is the highest in the land. With it, educated unemployment has also been rather high even though an average keralite is a compulsive migrant to distant lands and pastures new in search of employment. This State, inspite of its high rate of education, stands vertically divided on communal lines. The politics of the State during the last more than two decades has been played on grounds of short-term political expediency rather than long term national interests. When governmental favours are granted selectively to the communities and not uniformly to the people as a whole this is an invitation to communalism of a vicious variety. What lends an edge to communalism is very often the manner in which government decisions are taken with a view to favour a particular communal group. Such governmental dispensations and policy formulations have only helped to nourish and consolidate communal identities in Kerala. Thus we see in Kerala a stage in the evolution of communalism which is distinct from the rest of the country.

Kerala has been ruled by coalition governments almost uninterruptedly from 1969 onwards. The political compulsions of successive coalition governments have greatly helped communal and caste groups to consolidate their position among the people of their respective communities and castes by conferrring respectability and relevance to communal and caste consciousness. Several decisions of successive governments such as the formation of districts, creating of new Universities, applicability of laws and regulations, have all, in their respective ways, put a premium on communal demands and further accentuated the communal divide. Because of the decisive political leverage that the Muslims through the Muslim League and the Christians through the Kerala Congress, in which they form the dominant group, can exercise on the Congress or the communist parties, one of which invariably is the major coalition partner, it has come to be believed, and even accepted, that all governmental decisions are to be tailored to placate the communal groups in the coalition. The Kerala Congress has been controlling Finance and Law for over six years and Revenue and Education during the last three and a half years. The Muslim League controlled Education and Public Works for several years and has been controlling Industries, Public Works and Civil Supplies for the last three and a half years. The decisions of the government taken in these departments are invariably seen as communally motivated and as such prejudicial to the larger interests of the state as a whole. Some of the examples citied in support of these allegations are:

15 technical schools were sanctioned in 1986 at a cost of Rs. 6 crores even though this had not been provided for in the plan. This is seen by Hindu communalists as a favour extended by the Christian Education Minister to the Christian dominated Kerala Congress for their continued support to the Congress-led coalition.

Recently a move has been initiated to bring the two years in the 10+2 system under the administration of a Pre-Degree Board. This would mean separating it from the Universities under whose control this stage of the education has been until recently. This decision, according to one estimate, will result in 90% of the private institutions getting the responsibility for organizing the plus two courses. Most of these instiutions are reported to be controlled by the Christian community. The majority community has taken a communal stand on this issue and it is alleging that the Education Minister who is Christian has made this move to benefit the institutions belonging to his community. They are impervious to the fact that this move has been initiated as a direct consequence of the recently announced national policy on education. This unfortunate episode which had taken the form of an almost state-wide agitation is indicative of the degree of distrust that has come to characterise the relationship between the communities. The plus two course constitutes the qualifying course for admission to professional colleges. The majority community apprehends that the control of this crucial stage in education by another community would adversely affect the chances of its wards getting admission to the professional colleges. The implications are evident. It is sad that the suspicion between the communities should have assumed such distressing magnitude.

Dr. P.K. Gopala Krishnan who was the Chairman of the Committee on the Economic Affairs of the Kerala Pradesh Congress Committee (1) had written in 1986 a 'Note on communal parties, surrender politics and the deepening crisis of the coalition government in the state'. According to his note:

1) Kerala spends liberally on education. Even though there has been a fall in the rate of growth of the population, more than six hundred schools have been started during 1982-1986 in the private sector, two-thirds of which are under Christian management. According to one estimate, an expenditure of about Rs. 25 crores is incurred every year on surplus teachers. Currently the state government meets fully the expenditure incurred by the management on teachers' salaries. It is alleged that the pressure for starting schools is because of the financial interest that the school management has in the appointment of teachers. The management has been accused of taking large sums of money as bribe for teachers' appointments.

2) An ordinance which has been promulgated several times deals with making the law relating to cutting of trees from forests stricter. It has been alleged that the Muslim League is against the ordinance being converted into an Act as this would adversely affect such of them as have been benefitting so far by the prevailing laxity. It has been alleged that delaying the enactment of this Act was the specific concession that the Congress, which is the leading coalition partner, extended to the League to get the Congress nominee elected to the Rajya Sabha.

3) The Muslim League had decided to give pension to the Mukries (Muslim priests). They had therefore requested the government to contribute a substantial amount to the WAKF Board. Since the commitment would have been large and would have led to demands from other communities, the government did not agree to this. But on the eve of the Parliamentary elections in 1984, they insisted and got the government to contribute Rs. 15 lakhs. It was reported that this was objected to even by the Election Commission. Though the payment of pension has not been started, the Muslim League is accumulating the funds released by the government and it is expected that the pensions will be announced in due course. They have pressed and got an allotment of another Rs. 15 lakhs in 1985-1986 even though this had not been provided for in the state Budget.

In all such decisions, the gains from the issues sought to be settled or the benefits conferred do not extend to the community as a whole but are limited to placating the vested interests within that community. Even if the community as a whole stands to gain by such decisions, this does not make it any less invidious and discriminatory, stemming as it does from coercive politics. In fact, under the facade of serving the particular community s interests, it only compounds what is wrong.

All these various concessions are seen by the Hindus in particular as 'surrender politics' eating into the vitals of the political life and administration of the state. What is being resented is the partisan nature of the decisions and the manner in which they are brought about by coercive political pressure. These various instances have brought into the open Hindu communalism in its most militant form. In April 1986 two 'Hindu Sangamams' (conventions) were held, one each in Trivandrum and Cannanore. By all accounts, these conventions were most impressive and were conducted with a very high degree of organizational discipline. The Rashtriya Swayam Sewak Sangh (R.S.S.) chief, in the course of his address to these gatherings, had advised them to meet aggressively any attack on them physically or culturally.

One of the other aspects of Hindu revivalism has been the migration of Hindu members from the Marxist fold, a rare political phenomenon. It needs to be made clear at this stage that the rank and file of Kerala communists of whatever persuasion are not agnostics who consider religion as an opiate of the people. The communist ranks are composed preponderantly of Hindus, cutting across caste lines. Rightly or wrongly a number of them have come to believe that in the type of politics that is played in the state the interests of the majority community are getting sacrificed in the anxiety of the leading political parties to come to power or to stay in power. In the process, the Marxist Party which had a considerable cadre strength has suffered a severe jolt because of a large number of the members moving over to the R.S.S. which is considered a highly communal organisation. Hindus are beginning to feel that their interest would be safe only if they fought for it by organizing themselves on communal lines. A fallout from this trend has been the rise of a Hindu communal political party which calls itself as "Hindu Munnani". One of the surest indicators of the degree of growth of Hindu communalism is provided by the votes polled by the Bhartiya Janta Party in a Parliamentary constituency from Trivandrum during 1982. It had secured 7,806 votes. In the same constituency during the Parliamentary elections held in 1985, the Hindu 'Munnani' secured 1,10,449 votes. The figures are eloquent enogh to carry the message loud and clear.

Thus we have in Kerala all the three communities consolidating their respective positions on communal lines for a share in the distrubution of political power. The communal divide seems to be complete as of now and mutual provocation is also much in evidence between the Hindus and the Muslims. The youth in the state is far more affected by the communal virus than the elders. As a matter of fact the elders among both the Hindus and the Muslims continue to exercise a sobering and restraining influence on the youths of their respective communities. There are a number of training camps organized by the **R.S.S.** and the Students Islamic Movement of India (S.I.M.I.). There has been an increase in the number of Islamic cultural centres where indoctrination of Islam and communal consciousness is inculcated regularly. Following the second annual convention of the **S.I.M.I.** in January, 1986 there was a rash of Malayalam posters in several parts of the state. The heading of the posters in Malayalam would read something as follows when translated: "The liberation of India through Islam." The **R.S.S.** replied with a rash of posters the heading of which ran as follows: "The end of Islam in India". With such provocative slogans can violence be far behind?

One of the points which the Hindu communalists are agitated about is the rate of increase in the Muslim population of Kerala as shown by the 1981 Census. The decadal growth rate of population in Kerala in 1981 was only 19.24% compared to the national growth rate of 24.69%. The increase of Hindus of Kerala was 16.7%, of Christians 16.4% and of Muslims 29.6%. This records an increase of 13% in Muslim population over the two other communities, which is viewed with concern by the Hindu communalists.

There have been reports of large scale funds from abroad flowing to communal organizations. The number of Muslim orphanages run with the assistance of such funds has increased visibly. Those Muslim children whose parents cannot afford to look after them are sent to these orphanages. There have been reports not only about the large scale receipt of unaccounted funds but also their gross misuse by individuals and institutions.

That funds are being received from the Gulf countries by certain Muslim organisations has been alleged for some time. There is reason to believe that this is to some extent justified. The latest report refers to the activities of two Kuwaitis who had visited Kerala in the month of February, 1986 even though they had been debarred from visiting the State for their alleged role in funding an organisation involved in conversion and distribution of money among certain Muslim organisations. The circumstances of their visit to Kerala and the complicty of some Muslim League MLAs and state government functionaries are all the sort of elements in communal politics which do not augur well for the growth of secularism. Any group which draws on extra territorial support, introduces in the process foreign interest in what should strictly be a domestic affair. And this has an obvious bearing on national integrity.

The Act which seeks to govern and regulate receipt of foreign funds is more honoured in its breach than in observance. According to a report, there are 20 Christian and Muslim organisations each of which are receiving about Rs. 25 lakhs annually from abroad. Most of these contributions come through normal banking channels and are meant to be spent for legitimate purposes. Some of the funds received by the Islamic institutions are reportedly used for propagating fundamentalist ideas and for conversions. Inquiries into this, if at all made by the local police, are of a perfunctory nature. The explanation that the police offer for not wanting to come to grips with the problem in its several disturbing implications is that if they did anything in the nature of a full and purposeful investigation, taking it to its logical conclusion, they would inevitably come up against not only obstacles from interested groups and individuals in the government but may also suffer distinct damage to their professional prospects. That there is a large scale and gross violation of the law in the receipt and use of these funds received from abroad is a fact, going by what unimpeachable sources have to say on the subject. Unless therefore the requisite political will is forthcoming to closely inquire into the sources and manner of expenditure of the funds of these various institutions through an agency which is independent of the state government, nothing worthwhile is likely to come out. This is a matter which can bear closer and keener scrutiny.

One of the sources of funds is the operation of smugglers along the Kerala coast. Considering the nexus between the underworld and the communal forces whose spread and strength in fomenting and sustaining communal violence has been demonstrated again and again in Ahmedabad and even in Bombay, the smuggling operations have to be taken extremely seriously. A joint operation by the Income-tax and Enforcement Directorate authorities ought to be a regular feature, and the outcome continuously monitored, for worth while results.

There has been re-thinking among certain sections of the Marxist leadership in Kerala on the subject of aligning with communal parties. One of their leaders has recently made a policy statement to the effect that his party will not align itself with communal parties in future. But this is a realisation to which the party has come rather late in the day, chastened by being out of power for long and by the depletion of its ranks caused by the migration of the disenchanted members to the R.S.S. The real test will be when the Marxist or the Congress or any other national party is able to resist the pull of power, when what keeps it away from power is lack of a small support which can be had only by compromising with a communal group.

Kerala today represents a very crucial stage in the evolution of communalism and communal politics. This is the direction in which the country in its macro level will be heading if the current nexus between politics and communalism continues to grow and thrive as in Kerala. Though in the all-India setting, communal parties still do not enjoy the status of an arbiter of the political destiny of the nation, given time this stage may soon be behind us if the present trend is not consciously arrested. Kerala deserves to be treated as a warning to the rest of the country of the damage that communal politics can do to divide the people vertically into mutually conflicting groups. That there is no large scale overt violence on the surface in Kerala is not indicative of the absence of animosity or an unwillingness to strike. It has more to do with the character of the people, the geography of the habitat and the restraining and sobering influence of the elders who have been witnesses to the traditional peace between the communities over the years. But given the increasing economic pressures and the sharper communal divide one cannot say how long the tenuous peace will last in this atmosphere, in which the best who constitute the right thinking minority lack the courage of their convictions, and the communalised who constitute the majority are full of passionate intensities.

d) Visitors from Pakistan and Bangladesh

There is yet another factor which though by itself is in the nature of a human problem, tends to assume communal overtones in the prevailing circumstances of Kerala. There are about a thousand Pakistani nationals scattered over the districts of Cannanore, Mallapuram and Calicut. Many of them do not want to go back as they are not wanted in Pakistan where they feel that they are treated as second class citizens. Pakistan must have presented itself to these Kerala Muslims back in the early 1950s as a virgin land with plenty of job opportunities, just as the Gulf countries have been looked upon by Indians belonging to all communities in the recent past. Many of them regret their initial decision to have gone to Pakistan in search of better job prospects and in the process getting themselves declared as Pakistani citizens—a situation for which their illiteracy, ignorance and poverty had contributed in no small measure. But now if they want to stay back in Kerala because of family ties they are hit by the travel rules and restrictions that cover the citizens of the two countries. Many such Pakistani nationls who have been deported on grounds of overstay have infiltrated back to their original places in Kerala and have further overstayed. But even among this category there are now two types: those who have managed to acquire Indian citizenship and those who, even though located, have not been arrested and deported. The police will not be able to satistactorily explain the anomalous situation projected by the second type without embarassment to themselves. The obvious conclusion is that the police may have been told to keep their hands off these persons by political party leaders in general, and in particular by the Muslim League legislators who wield considerable political and administrative influence in the coalition politics of Kerala. In any case the problem presented by these Pakistanis gets mixed up with the coalition politics of Kerala to which it inevitably lends a communal edge.

If one takes into account the number of visiting Pakistanis who remain untraced in India at any given point of time, it becomes easy to conclude that there could be enough agent provocateurs among them to create problems between the communities which would in turn subserve geo-political and anti-India interests.

It can be stated authentically that since 1980, the average number of Pakistanis visiting India would be above two lakhs, of whom at least about seven to eight thousand remain behind every year and go underground. The figures of Pakistani arrivals and those who go untraced in the country have increased since the 70s.

The large number of Pakistanis visiting India has to be viewed in the context of the thousands of families which got divided during the partition and parts of which continue to be in both the countries. The majority of the visitors are genuinely motivated by sentimental considerations and are not interested in politics of any type that keeps the two countries apart. If anything, they would like to see the countries coming closer because of the several cultural ties which continue to be common between them. What should be a matter for concern is, when some of these visitors overstay and worse, they become untraced and go underground. Thus the persons who have remained untraced over the years are those that constitute the security hazard.

Some of the little known facts about Pakistani nationals visiting India are: often a number of them furnish incomplete or false addresses of their relations in India. Many do not report their arrivals and/or departures to the police, which is a statutory requirement. Quite a number of them secretly visit places which they are not authorised to visit under their visa stipulations. A number of them have been known to have torn off their Passports and merged with the local people. Some of them had tried to pass off as Indian citizens, and have moved the Courts to frustrate actions taken by the authorities to deport them out of the country. The problem of untraced Pakistani nationals is extremely serious particularly in the State of Bihar, Gujarat, Madhya Pradesh, Rajasthan, Kerala and Uttar Pradesh. Apart from the entry of Pakistanis on valid documents, hundreds of them infiltratre through the borders of Rajasthan and Punjab. They are mostly smugglers. They indulge in crimes such as dacoity and cattle lifting. They also run missions for Pakistani Intelligence Agencies and many of them have been known to have merged and settled down as Hindus in India but are doing espionage work for Pakistan.

In February, 1987 the Chief Judicial Magistrate of Jamnagar had awarded four years rigorous imprisonment and a fine to a Pakistani national for illegally staying in India and pretending to be an Indian national. The Magistrate had observed in his judgement that the offender was holding a Pakistani passport and identify card. Yet he had got his name entered in the voters list on the basis of which he had also voted in the last assembly elections in Gujarat. He had also managed to get a ration card.

The Chief Minister of Gujarat informed the State Assembly in February, 1987 that as many as 303 Pakistans had been undergoing imprisonment in the jails in the state for the last one year on various charges.

The seizure of 31 kgs. of gold in Delhi on 20th April 1986 from the house of a person who was trying to pass off as an Indian national by name Sunil led to the discovery that Sunil was a Pakistani national living under an assumed Hindu name and indulging in smuggling. What he and his ilk may be contributing to the communal virus in India can only be guessed.

The then Minister for Internal Security said in Parliament on 24th April 1986 that during the three months preceeding the statement, 44 Pak intruders and spies were shot dead by our security forces, and 1,333 Pak intruders and 13 spies were arrested on the Pakistan border. The number of persons illegally crossing from Pakistan to India and vice versa apprehended by the security forces during the six months following Ist October 1985 was 8,547. This was at a time when vigilance on the Indo-Pak border by our security forces was supposed to be at its peak. This should give an idea of the dimension of the problems of smuggling and related activities by Pak nationals who have necessarily their collaborators on this side of the border.

Ever since the trouble in Punjab got intensified and in particular immediately before operation Blue Star there had been reports of Pakistani nationals being found in the Punjab going about disguised as Sikhs. There could only be one motive for their presence under the prevailing conditions and that is to fuel anti-national activities in Punjab, which is once again an integral part of Pakistan's political objectives. Pakistan is not likely to relax till it has exacted the price according to its reckoning for the dismemberment that it had suffered, and for which it holds India responsible. The problem that we are facing in Punjab has to be seen in this perspective. The implications can be sinister and will have to be faced.

In this context the observations of Arun Nehru in Parliament in April, 1986 while speaking on the situation in Punjab are relevant. He said: In the last six months 20 to 30 terrorists had been caught (Mr. Nehru had said that he was not giving the exact figures deliberately) and their clear link with Pakistan had been established; that he had all the details of names, locations, training schedules and the type of assistance Pakistan had given to these terrorists; that in the past two and a half months nearly 2,200 were apprehended on the western border, of whom 2,050 had been pushed back and the remaining handed over to the Punjab Police.

About the complicity of Pakistan in terrorist activities in Punjab there should be no doubt. According to a report(7), Lt. Gen. Mujib-ur-Rehman, who at the time of reporting was Pakistan's Secretary for Sports and Culture and an American trained specialist in psychological warfare, was incharge of supervising a specialised outfit to undertake subversive operations in Punjab. He was the same man who according to reliable reports handed over a German Walther pistol to the Sikh hijacker of an Indian Airlines plane in August, 1984. Interpol had confirmed that the German pistol recovered from the hijackers was purchased by the Pakistani government from the Company, Walther Gmbh of West Germany.

India's then External Affairs Minister P. Shiv Shankar answering questions at a joint meeting with the national foreign policy committee on U.S. foreign policy and the Indian Chamber of Commerce in New York on 25th September, 1986 is reported to have said that the Indian government had given 'day-by-day and hour-by-hour' evidence to Islamabad to show how the terrorists who are operating in Punjab and elsewhere in India were being trained in Pakistan, how weapons were being supplied to them and how people, many disgiused as Sikhs, were being infiltrated into India. In the context of such overwhelming evidence from the most authentic source, about the complicity and contribution of Pakistan to the problems of communalism in India, every visiting Pakistani who does not conform to the visa restrictions and regulations, and especially if he gets lost and goes underground, is a serious security hazard.

The problem has also to be viewed in the context of the constant and continuing influx of Bangladesh nationals in large numbers. They merge easily because of the language affinity with the Bengalis. This subject has to be viewed in national terms rather than in merely narrow political terms in the context of winning or losing local elections. Unless and until this subject is viewed by divorcing it from the election politics of interested politicians in the States affected, this problem can result in violence. Anything short of this will merely be politics of expediency with consequences which will echo far into the future.

Ashim Mukhopadhyay(8) had furnished several details about the influx of Bangladeshis into West Bengal. In the town of Dhulian in Murshidabad district, against the town's population of 24,000 the number of ration cards issued was 30,000. There are more such places. In 1985, the number of Bangladeshi infiltrants who were pushed back by the Border Security Force on the West Bengal border was put at 30,000. The number who might have escaped detection can only be guessed.

According to the figures of the 1981 Census, while West Bengal's total population had risen by 23.17% since the Census of 1971, the population of the border districts viz. 24 Parganas rose by 27.1%, West Dinajpur by 29.3%, Darjeeling by 31%, Cooch Bihar by 25%, Nadia by 33%, Murshidabad by 25.76% and Malda by 26%.

West Bengal has a border extending over 2,100 kilometres through paddy fields, rivers and rivulets and even cutting through houses. Fencing a border of this type is going to be an extremely difficult job. What is worse, the maintenance of this fencing may well cost more than even the inital cost of fencing. The Border Security Force outposts stretched along the border number about 300. The nature of the terrain does not permit an uninterrupted field of vision. The guarding as of now is clearly inadequate, if we are to go by the increase in infiltration. According to Ashis K. Biswas (9) category-wise figures of

Bangladeshis who were arrested and pushed back by the Border Security Force and other agencies in 1983 and 1984 were:

Table 5

Bangladeshis arrested and pushed back at the West Bengal Bangladesh Border

1983: Arrested and pushed back by the BSF		By other agencies
Hindus :	2,571	1,347
Muslims:	6,634	10,406
Burmese:	184	401
Pakistanis:	159	150
1984: Arrested and pushed back by the BSF		Others
Hindus:	1,887	2,674
Muslims:	7,790	9,325
Burmese:	27	68
Pakistanis:	9	Nil

The figures of people who had entered West Bengal with valid entry documents but are reported to have stayed back is believed to be over 50,000. They cannot be traced because the addresses in their documents were apparently false. According to the Inspector General of Police, Border Security Force. Calcutta who addressed a Press Conference in 1985, the number of people from Bangladesh who had crossed over without the benefit of legal formalities would be over 40,000 in Greater Calcutta alone. All these figures will assume significance in the years to come.

In recent years there have been infiltrations into India by those among several streams of migrants from Bangladesh, who are known as Bihar Muslims. They were the victims of Hindu communalism of the pre-partition days. Since they could not l esh with the Punjabi Muslims of West Pakistan, they went to East Pakistan where the Bengali Muslims indentitied them with the aggressive and overlording West Pakistan Muslims. When Bangladesh seceded from Pakistan, though there was an understanding that Pakistan would take back the Bihari Muslims, this never materialised. Nor did the Bangladeshis assimilate them. On the countrary, the Bangladeshis did everything possible to make it difficult for the Bihari Muslims to continue in Bangladesh. The result has been that these Bihari Muslims have been infiltrating back to the state to which they belonged earlier. This can be another source of communal trouble in Bihar.

e) Muslim Personal Law

One of the points of conflicts in recent months which has been agitating a section of the Muslims is their fear that their Personal Law is being interfered with because of the Supreme Court judgement in the Shah Bano case.

I owe an explanation for dealing with this sensitive subject of the Muslim Personal Law at some length. Let me say at the outset that I am not going into the merits or the demerits of the Muslim Personal Law as I am just not competent to do so. The reason why I have drawn on the writings of some of the eminent Muslim scholars is only to indicate that there is a volume of progressive Muslim opinion in India which demands some changes which would involve a little departure from the Muslim Personal Law as construed by the Muslim orthodox section. When this demand is resisted successfully by the orthodox section of the Muslims, it gives rise to an impression, whether rightly or wrongly among the non-Muslims in India, that the section of the Muslims who are averse to the idea of change have had their way on matters in which even the other Islamic countries have themselves advocated and adopted wide ranging changes. This has created an impression among a section of the Hindus about the ascendency of Muslim fundamentalism, and its ability to influence government's action. These sections of the Hindus in turn have tried to match this with their own brand of strident and aggressive Hindu communalism. My purpose in dealing with this subject therefore is limited to the extent of recognising the existence of this confrontation, as it is contributing towards vitiating an atmosphere which already stands charged with communalism. The peace of any place largely depends on how an average man perceives a problem, a situation, or even a community's behaviour. What one perceives as truth has no relevance to what the truth in fact is, in a complex social context. In a plural society like the one that we are living in, how each community perceives the other community becomes a factor contributing to peace as well as strife.

Muslim Personal Law has undergone vast changes in the different Muslim countries such as Tunisia, Pakistan and others. Pakistan enacted the Muslim Family Law of 1961 giving effect to a number of progressive demands of Pakistani women. According to one of its provisions divorce must be carried out under judicial control and it is no longer a purely private unilateral act. It has been reported that when Gen. Zia declared martial-law with the support of the so-called fundamentalists, they demanded as a price for their support the repeal of the Family Laws Ordinance. The opposition to such a demand was so very vociferous and widespread from some of the leading women members of Pakistan society that Gen. Zia had to yield. It is said that his wife told him that if he did not scrap the repealing Bill, she would herself publicly associate with the demonstrations against it. Gen. Zia bowed to the women's protests and scrapped the repealing Bill(10).

Muslim scholars from all over the country collected at Srinagar on 7th October, 1985 to participate in the Shariat week. According to the scholars, the Supreme Court judgement in the Shah Bano case had misinterpreted the Koran and ignored the traditions of the Prophet. Sulaiman Sait, President of the Indian Union Muslim League was of the view that there is a deliberate attempt to create conflict between Muslim men and women and a conspiracy to weaken the communty as a whole. G.M. Banatwala, MP, said the Muslim Personal Law is an inseparable part of their religion.

The Supreme Court judgement on the Shah Bano case provoked divergent reactions among the Muslims themselves. Some of the leaders of the Muslim community in Kerala led by one P.V. Shaukat Ali formed an Islamic Shariat Board which declared that the judgement was not against the Islamic Shariat or the Koran. As against this, the Students Islamic Movement in India warned that Muslims in Maharashtra would observe Republic Day as "Black Day" if the Supreme Court verdict on the Shah Bano case was not overruled.

What is at issue is the dilemma of the state in reconciling the concept of justice and equality in a plural society with the sectional demands of a community based on religion, which go counter to this equality. The Personal Law provides a focal point which, to a section of the Muslims, is what alone will preserve their separate identity as a community. Quite a significant segment of the Muslim men and women do not subscribe to this idea.

M.R.A. Baig, who was private secretary to late M.A. Jinnah till 1940 observes(11): "There is ample evidence that Mohammed Himself never intended that social development of Muslims should stop when Revelation ceased on his death.... On the contrary Mohammed's concept of future Islam has been clearly brought out by the great authority on Islam, Syed Amir Ali, when in THE SPIRIT OF ISLAM he wrote: 'the Great Teacher with His keen anxiety and breadth of views perceived and one may say foretold that the time would come when the accidental and temporary regulations would have to be different from the permanent and general. You are in an age, he declared, in which if you abandon 1/10th of what is being ordered, you will be ruined. After this a time will come when he who shall observe 1/10th of the now ordered will be redeemed.'

Writing about the Muslim Personal Law the late M.C. Chagla, who had been a Chief Justice and our Foreign Minister(1973) observed: "Consider the attitude of the government to the question of a Uniform Civil Code. Although the directive principles of the state enjoins such a Code, government has refused to do anything about it on the plea that the minorities will resent any attmept at imposition... I wholly and emphatically disagree with this view. The Constitution is binding on every one, majority and minority; and if the Constitution contains a directive, that directive must be accepted and implemented. Jawaharlal showed great strength and courage in getting the Hindu Reform Bill passed, but he accepted the policy of laissez faire where the Muslims and other minorities were concerned. I am horrified to find that in my country while monogamy has been made the law for the

Hindus, Muslims can still indulge in polygamy. It is an insult to womanhood; and Muslim women, I know, resent this discrimination between Muslim women and Hindu women."

According to M.C. Chagla, "Government's policy of constantly harping on minority status and minority rights comes in the way of national unity and emphasises the difference between the majority community and the minority. Ofcourse, it may serve well as a vote catching device to win Muslim votes but I do not believe in sacrificing national interests in order to get temporary party benefits.... The Congress government has also often followed what I can only call the old British policy of communalism."

Tahir Mohammed writes (13) : "Islamic laws of marriage, divorce, succession are treated by the general run of Muslims as an integral part of their religion. They sincerely believe that the Muslim Personal Law is co-terminus with the Koran and the Sunna.... Muslim Personal Law both in India and elsewhere has in its fabric much more man-made than scriptural rules..... All the great doctors of law, whose interpretations of and deductions from certain Koranic and Sunnite text form the basis of Muslim Personal Law, had declared that their words were neither final or binding even on their contemporaries, to say nothing of the future generations. It is in keeping with these facts about the nature and dynamism of Muslim Personal Law that it has been reformed by a large number of Muslim countries.... In fact, the various reforms needed can easily be introduced in Muslim Personal Law without going outside the broad Islamic framework."

M.R.A. Baig writes in his book: "No one has drawn attention to the anachronisms in Islam more clearly than Mohabubul Hok, who wrote in an article: "The idea of implementing the Koranic laws in the modern state is simply an absurdity. It is either foolishness or hypocrisy to conceive an Islamic state of Islamic culture today as Islam is adumberated in the Koran. Neither the Koran nor the Sunna permits a Muslim to repeal any law or principle of the Koran... We have already said that the religion of a community is the totality of those laws and principles which uphold or seek to uphold that community. The religion of Islam is inconceivable without the Koran... Without the Koranic laws, an Islamic state exists nowhere except in the mind of the fools or on the lips of the hypocrites." (14).

Baig continues : "A lot of re-thinking has to take place, but who will do it? The Ulema claims that any Ijma or Ijtihad is their God given function. They have made no move since independence and show no sign of doing so. Nor can it be expected of them. In poor economic circumstances and rarely educated in any subject but theology, they may know the Koran by heart but little of what is going on in the world.... Yet they claim a sort of 'dyarchy' with Personal Law as a 'reserved subject'. Besides even they cannot have it both ways. If the Koranic provisions governing polygamy, divorce, inheritance etc. cannot be amended, then the provisions governing amputation of hand, chastisement of women, etc. must be strictly complied with. If however, it is permissible to disregard certain provisions, then there can be no doctrinal objection to the amendment of others. Muslim Indian are, therefore in the unenviable position of being unable to be good citizens and practising Muslims simultaneously. This is their dilemma. There is no way out of this dilemma except reforms of the social element of the moral social system which in its totality is Islam. Muslim Indians have, therefore, to decide whether they will continue to live as hypocrites or whether they will reconcile the anachronisms and anomalies of Islam with the India of today, legitimatise the inevitable changes and live in India with a free conscience and as good citizens. The Ulema will do nothing to resolve their dilemma and it is for the thinking Muslims to take up the challenge. If they refuse to move, and signs of movement are difficult to discern, then Parliament, which is of all Indians, by all Indians and for all Indians, irrespective of caste, cred, or community, must move for them. Democracy has a duty to perform to social progress and must never tolerate social stagnation."

Some of the Muslim wnmen who had suffered the rigours of divorce and the members of the Muslim Satya Shodhak

Mandal, Pune and other social organisations made a fervent plea on 25th February 1986 to the Prime Minister for the reconsideration of the proposed Muslim Women (Protection of rights on divorce) Bill which has since been passed by both the houses of Parliament in the Budget session of 1986, and become law.

That a section of the community was strongly against the proposed Bill was more than amply demonstrated by the resignation of Arif Mohammed Khan, who was a Minister of State in the Central Cabinet in protest against the Bill. Without going into the merits of the resignation of Arif Mohammed Khan, one cannot resist observing that at a time when shoddy practices, compromised standards, communalised politics and rampant cynicism have become an integral part of our political culture, Arif Mohammed Khan by sacrificing his high office for what he thought was a principle worth standing up for has shown himself up as a thread of scarlet in an otherwise faded fabric of public life.

f) Educational Profile of Muslims

In the context of the Personal Laws the backwardness of Muslims in the educational fied is very relevant. Ahmed Rashid Sherwani (15), who is an authority on the state of education among the Muslims, in an article gave the following figures which speak for themselves:

The population of Delhi in 1978 was about 54 lakhs of whom Muslims were 5.1 lakhs. The number of students who appeared for the Class X Board examination in 1978 was 54000 or one thousand per lakh of population or one percent. The number of Muslim students appearing for the secondary board examination in 1978 from Delhi was just 907. This works out to a little more than 0.2% of Delhi's Muslim population. Out of all the 54000 students who appeared, 67% passed, while of the Muslims who appeared only 46% passed. Out of the total of 54000 about 4000 got first division. Out of 907 Muslims only 27 got first division. This works out to about 0.7% of all the first divisioners. This would mean that if 1000 first divisioners compete for admission to any good course of study, just about 7 of them are likely to be Muslims. In Bihar 250 per lakh of Muslims appeared in the entrance examination in 1978 and in Uttar Pradesh it was 125. In Delhi it was only 180 per lakh. In quite a number of places, the Muslims have been going to schools run by their own society though quite a small percentage of them have also been joining the general stream.

The very low percentage of Muslim students going up for higher education is probably also due to the fact that they are content with the Madrassa type of education and do not pursue higher studies either due to want of interest or due to strong economic reason. The Madrassa system of education has certain built-in characteristics. In the words of A.R. Sayed of Jamia Milia Islamia, Delhi (16): "Some scholars have pointed out that behind the conservatism of the Ulema lies the traditional Madrassa seminary system of Ulema education which is the pivotal institution for the continuation of the Islamic tradition. In India the training imparted in most Muslim seminaries has managed to remain stagnant due to adherence to what is known as the Nizami syllabus whose style and content continue to be more or less the same as formulated at the end of 17th Century by an Indian theological scholar Mulla Nizamuddin (1669 to 1748)... Suffice it to say that in contemporary society there are few educational anachronisms that can rival Madrassas in India... Thus when one bears in mind the nature and ethos of the Madrassas and the socio-economic background of its recruits, one sees that it would be futile, on purely sociological grounds for anyone to expect any initiative or concurrence for any change in the Muslim Personal Law from these custodians of custom and tradition. The Ulemas find a ready audience among these semi-literate, anxious and insecure people for whom religion is the only possession that matters and in which they are therefore unwilling for any compromise... Thus in India the relative backwardness of the Muslim community has given the Ulemas a large number of allies. Like the Mandarins of Imperial China, the Ulema too are afraid of change and equate change with crisis. This fear of their s they skillfully transfer to the lower social strata and win them over in favour of stagnation."

Table 6

The number of Madrassas in some of the districts in Bihar in 1985 with a significant Muslim population:

Name of districts in order of percentage of Muslims	No. of Madrassas
Purnea	454
Madhubani	103
Katihar	68
Santhalpargana	68
Darbhanga	61
Bhagalpur	47
West Champaran	37
Sitamarhi	37

In the context of all that has been quoted from the writings of different Muslim scholars which has a bearing on the attidue and conditions of the Muslims in independent India, it seems rather strange that Syed Shahabuddin, MP(17), should attribute the evils and ills that Muslim society in India is suffering from, to machinations of the majority community. He observes: "The Muslim community is in a state of physical, cultural and political insecurity. The prevailing self-image is largely that of deprivation, discrimination and helplessness of being surrounded by the rising forces of Hindu chauvinism and of being the object of Hindu anxiety to assimilate or to absorb it within its fold... After 1971 the year which I have called the psychological watershed, the Muslims in India appear to have made their choice and made a conscious effort towards adjustment with their environment... If educational backwardness persists it is largely due to their relative economic backwardness, non-establishment of government institutions in adequate numbers in Muslim villages and

Mohallas, virtual banishment of Urdu from the educational syllabus in the Hindi-belt, Hindu overtones found in text books particularly of languages and history, deliberate Hinduisation of school culture and insecurity about employment."

The statistics, however, speak a different story. An average Muslim in the rural areas sees modern education as a threat to Islamic values and he prefers to send his children to Madrassas and Maqtabas, which while teaching them about Islam do not equip them with the knowledge required for their socio-economic upward mobility.

N.C. Saxena, of the Indian Administrative Service (18), who was the Revenue Secretary in Uttar Pradesh and who at the time was on deputation to the Government of India had written an article under the title: "Public Employment and Educational Backwardness among Muslims in India". Some of the conclusions he arrived at are being reproduced below:

Field data was collected from 45 districts, in 12 states spread over the country where Muslim population was significant. The number of Muslims in the surveyed districts was 17.32%. The number of Muslims in the elementary schools in these 45 districts was 12.39%. In a similar survey done in 38 districts spread over eleven states which had a Muslim population of 18.56% the Muslim enrolment in secondary school was 10.70%. In high schools spread over eleven states where the population was 12%, the percentage of Muslim enrolment was only 4%. In the 12th class spread over five Boards where the Muslim population was 10.30%, the Muslim enrolment was only 2.49%. In the Engineering classes spread over nine Universities which had a Muslim population of 12.44%, the enrolment was 3.41%. In 12 Medical college spread over an area where the Muslim population was 9.55%, the Muslim enrolment was only 3.44%. The figures of population percentage referred to are based on the 1971 Census whereas the students' enrolment from which the percentage has been worked out relates to the year 1981-1982. The conclusion that can be drawn is that at the high schools and higher levels Muslims are only 25% of the other communities in their enrolment.

Saxena has quoted in the course of his study the following observations of Sherwani on the subject of Muslim education and employment.

"And all this while, the Muslim leaders and the Hindu secular leaders have been telling Muslims they are not getting jobs because of discrimination. I do not deny discrimination. We Indians are the most discriminating people on earth... But the position is that Muslims are not even giving anyone a chance to discriminate against them in worthwhile services. Anyone can discriminate against Muslims only when they qualify and compete. How many Muslims are competing? This no one tells, neither the Muslim leaders nor the secular Hindu leaders who go about as the best friends of the Muslims."

Saxena quoting S. Nazeem A. Zaidi (19) observes:
"In the last five years no Muslim candidate secured a position in the merit list of Class X and XII examinations conducted by the Central Board of Higher Secondary Education, which has a network of schools spread throughout the country with 16 branches in other Muslim countries. In the merit list of XII Class for the 1983 examination out of the first 70 students, a Scheduled Tribe candidate got 51st position, but there was no Muslim name in the first 70."

It is significant that Muslims studying in Hindi medium schools did much better than Muslims who studied in minority Urdu medium institutions. Not only was the overall percentage of Muslims better in Hindi medium schools but the number of first divisioners from such schools was higher as compared to Urdu medium schools.

On the basis of information collected from the Minority Commission, Saxena has observed that out of the students who appeared at the B.A. examination of Delhi University in

1980, only 1.47% were Muslims as against the Muslim population in Delhi of 9.4%. In B.Com., B.Sc., and Engineering, their number in Delhi Unversity was 1.35%, 1.30% and 1.04% respecitively.

The Hamdard Education Society did an all India survey of 430 Muslim-managed schools and 44 Muslim-managed degree colleges in 1983. According to the figures quoted by Saxena, the number of non-Muslim students in these institutions rose from 3.7% at the primary level to 59.6% at the graduate level while in the case of the Muslim boys the percentage declined from 56.3 at the primary level to 32.1 at the graduate level. The percentage of Muslim girls also declined from 40 at the primary level to 8.3 at the graduate level.

The conclusions arrived at by Saxena on the basis of his study are broadly as follows.

1) At the high schools and intermediate levels which are crucial for employment purposes, the percentage of Muslims is roughly 1/4th to 1/3rd of what it should be according to their population.
2) The drop-out rate of Muslim students keeps going up progressively as they move up in the educational level compared to the non-Muslim students.
3) The Muslim students did better in non-denominational schools than in Muslm-managed schools.
4) Educational institutions managed by Muslims attract at the higher levels more non-Muslims than Muslims.
5) The number of first divisioners among the Muslim candidates is vey low.
6) Schools and colleges tend to be located in Hindu majority localities.

g) Muslims' Share in Employment

The number of Muslim Indian Administrative Service Officers up to 1981 was 116 out of 3883 which works out to 2.99%. In the Indian Police Service out of 1753, there were 50 which works to 2.85%. In 1317 branches of Banks, upto 1980 the number of Muslim employees was 2.18%.

Data collected from 83 employment offices spread over fourteen states show that out of a total of 41.88 lakh registrations. 2.82 lakhs were Muslims constituting 6.77%. Out of 1,16,305 placements effected, 6,170 were Muslims constituting 5.31%. In 57 employment exchanges spread over eleven states, the total number of Muslim candidates was 2.50 lakhs out of which 50% were with qualifications below matric, 37.25% with qualifications of matric/higher secondary, 6.71% with degree qualifications, 0.83% with post-graduate qualifications and 5.15% with professional qualification. Source: (20) Saxena.

Muslims in Public Sector Undertakings

From the Annual Reports of 82 Public Sector Undertakings of the Central Government, it was revealed that out of 449 Directors, only 21(4.2%) were Muslims and out of 13,916 senior officers, only 321(2.32%) were Muslims.

Muslims in State Judiciary

Muslim representation among the judicial officers in some of the state governments was as follows in 1981:

Table 7
Representation of Muslims in Judiciary

Name of the state	Total	Muslims	Percentage
Andhra Pradesh	327	31	9.48
Assam	155	31	20.00
Bihar	1060	70	8.74
Gujarat	412	36	8.74
Haryana	32	2	6.25
Karnataka	223	16	7.17
Kerala	249	19	7.63
Maharashtra	614	19	3.09
Orissa	264	2	0.76
Uttar Pradesh	1144	64	5.59
West Bengal	418	13	3.11
Total	4898	303	6.19

Muslims in Competitive Examinations

In order to assess the performance of Muslim candidates in competitive examinations, data collected from some of the State Public Service Commissions were as in the following table:

Table-8

Muslims' performance in competitive examinations held during 1978-1980 (Source Saxena)

Name of the Commission	Muslim percentage in total		
	Who appeared	Called for interview	Selected
Andhra Pradesh	4.27	3.37	3.06
Tamil Nadu	3.95	3.91	4.63
UP Combined State Services	8.46	1.21	2.46
Bihar Combined State Services	4.54	6.36	7.30
Madhya Pradesh	2.89	1.77	1.70

On 3rd July, 1983 the Staff Selection Commission conducted an examination to fill about 7,000 vacancies in various grades of central services. Nearly 6,000 candidates opted to take the examination in Aligarh. It was conducted there in 13 sub-centres. A survey of 5 of these sub-centres revealed that the percentage of candidates from the Aligarh Muslim University ranged from 2 to 4.2 with the average of 3.3. The rest were all graduates from other institutions. This was the state of affairs in Aligarh itself. Commenting on this, Naseem A. Zaidi(21) has observed: "The attitude of Muslim parents and guardians and their approach to education make a real difference. The children are not inspired to aspire for higher academic standars and are not reminded of their present tasks and future targets. Muslim leadership in India (if there is one) is always obsessed with non-issues with the objective of projecting its own image in the community without making any serious effort to reform it. Since independence the community has produced numerous self-styled and self-centred political leaders, but no social reformer worth the name."

Information about some of the licences granted by the state government is as follows:

Table 9
Muslim share in Licences
(Source: Saxena)

Category	Sample	Total no.	Muslims	Percentage
Fair Price Shops	73 districts 14 states	3.5 lakhs	0.24 lakhs	6.97
Other/Shops Licences	18 districts in 9 states	1.94 lakhs	0.24 Lakhs	12.25
Truck Permits	62 districts in 13 states	1,06,110	18038	17.00
Bus Permits	—do—	26,990	4524	17.40
Auto Rickshaws/ Taxis	—do—	82,000	17000	20.20
Sale of houses constructed by government	22 districts	1,21,447	3478	2.86

Muslims in Private Sector Jobs

Employment of Muslims in some of the private sector undertakings was as follows:

Table 10
Muslims in Private Sector Employment

Name of the undertaking	Muslim Share in (percentage)		
	Executive Cadre	Supervisory Cadre	Workers Cadre
TISCO	4.1	5.6	10.30
Texmaco	Nil	0.3	4.4
Mafatlal	Nil	1.72	3.53
Calico	0.68	N.A.	10.2
Mahindra & Mahindra	1.48	2.25	5.02
Orkay	3.3	3.00	11.9
J.K. Industries	2.63	2.28	5.41
Indian Explosives	Nil	2.73	7.09

Data collected from 145 private enterprises in 33 districts of 12 states show that the Muslim share in supervisory non-technical jobs and in the category of workers was respectively 8.28% and 7.93%. Their share in technical supervisory posts was, however, only 2.49% (164 out of 6,622 posts) (22)

Inspite of the foregoing statistics, when Muslim leaders repeat charges of being discriminated against, one wonders whether this is due to lack of knowledge of facts, or their anxiety to pressurise the government into giving a protected status to Muslims for employment purposes. A self-conscious and sulking religous minority is prone to be exploited by the frustrated elitė among them, who will provide leadership on the basis of an ideological orientation. Such efforts would only further aggravate the communal problem and alienate the community yet more from the mainstream of national life.

Statistics relating to the backwardness of Muslims in the field of education should be a matter of concern for all who are concerned with the welfare of the country generally. The disinclination of weaker sections among the Muslims to make use of the available educational facilities could be mainly due to economic reasons. Many of them who may be engaged in traditional occupations such as artisans and the like may be unwilling to forego the meagre daily income that they may be earning should they get diverted to schools on a regular basis. It is worth exploring whether a system of education could be devised which while permitting the pursuit of traditional avocation could also provide for a few hours of regular education.

It is absolutely imperative that the spread of education among Muslims, both male and female, embraces a very much larger section than it does at present. One can understand the economic constraints of the poorer sectios among the Muslims. According to one of the surveys, more than 70% of Indian Muslims live below the poverty line. This is understandable considering the large scale and pitiless exploitation of Muslim artisans who have specialised in several arts and crafts such as carpet weaving, lock making, brassware manufacture, zari works, bangle making, leather and 'chikan work and others. The wages that are paid to these talented workers are exteremly low for which both Muslim and Hindu employers and middlemen are equally responsible. There has been no effort to organise these several thousand workers through cooperatives and trade unions, with the result that they are not able to get their rightful wages to which they are entitled. Shri. Asgar Ali Engineer (23) writing in his book: "Indian Muslims: A study of the minority problem in India", deplores the fact that 'the Muslim leadership' in India is guilty of callously neglecting the real problem of the Muslim masses. He has been critical of the fact that the vast funds which have been coming to the Muslims from the Arab countries have not neen utilized to run modern educational institutions for Muslims. He has pointed out: "The Muslim leadership is no less responsible for keeping the Muslim problem politically alive as it helps them in making opportunistic alliances, thus enabling them to reach the corridors of power". He has criticised the Muslim leadership for bringing up only issues which are of an emotional nature such as the Muslim Personal Law, the status of Urdu, the Minority character of the

Aligarh Muslim University and the like. Such issues get high lighted and this is always at the expense of the genuine problems of the Muslim masses. Agitating on such emotional issues while neglecting the basic problems of the Muslim masses has not been without its impact in fuelling communalism among the Muslims.

According to Article 45 of the Constitution : "The state shall endeavour to provide, within a period of ten years from the commencement of this Constitution, for free and compulsory education for all children until they complete the age of 14 years." Article 46 reads as follows: "The state shall promote with special care the educational and economic interests of the weaker sections of the people and in particular, of the Scheduled Castes and the Scheduled Tribes, and shall protect them from social injustice and all forms of exploitation".

While Section 45 is not being complied with rigorously, Section 46 is being followed with regard to the Scheduled Castes and Scheduled Tribes. But the application of these articles to all the weaker sections including Muslims leaves something to be desired. In view however of the importance that education has in bringing into being an enlightened society in which violence will be reduced to the minimum, we cannot afford to ignore the imperatives contained in Article 45 and 46 of the Constitution. Article 46 is as relevant to the weaker sections among the Muslims as it is to the Scheduled Castes and Scheduled Tribes.

h) Muslims and Elections

There are 14 districts in India with a Muslim majority and 114 districts where the population is 15% and above, against the national figure of 12%. There has been an increase in the number of Muslim MPs in Parliament in the 80s. There were 32 Muslim MPs in the 1977 Parliament, 45 Muslim MPs in 1980 and 42 Muslim MPs in the 1984/1985 Parliament. There are 120 Parliamentary and 700 Assembly constituencies all over the country in which the voting pattern of Muslims could be a decisive factor in tipping the balance one way or the other. Hence the political parties make a speical mention in their respective election manifestoes of what they want to do for the Muslims in the event of their getting elected. The considerations that go into the calculations of the average Muslim voter are the short-term rather than long-term interests, and the extent to which the candidate himself is sympathetic to the cause of the Muslims. The Muslims are keenly conscious of the extent to which they can influence the composition of a state legislature and their leadership understandably has not been averse to advising them on the lines which will best suit the interest of the community. The nature and content of the advice thus has a lot to do with the communal outlook of the leaders themselves. The position as of now generally is for the Muslims to align with different political parties with a view to be able to play the role of pressure groups within the party. In West Bengal and Tripura, Muslims have been known to have voted on ideological considerations in favour of the leftist parties, though in Kerala they have generally voted in favour of the Muslim League. The Itthad-Ul-Muslimeen in Andhra Pradesh had done extremely well in the Hyderabad Corporation elections of 1986. They are the single largest party with 38 seats in a house of 100. This means that depending on the circumstances, sections of Muslims would not be averse to keep their political identity separate from other parties.

Emerging out of the anti-reservation agitation in Gujarat is a trend which, though it has been there in certain places in the country in a more or less dormant form, is now coming to the surface. During the riots in Ahmedabad a slogan that was raised was: "Muslim-Harijan Bhai Bhai". The implications of this should be evident to anyone who is a student of communal politics in India. There was also a move by one of the leading names in the smuggling world of Bombay to form a political alliance between a section of the Muslims and the Dalits to fight the 1984-1985 Parliament and Assembly elections in Maharashtra, as a counter to the other political parties. A party called Dalit Muslim Suraksha Mahasang was also formed in 1984 in Bombay. For whatever reason, this political alliance of convenience did not take off the ground. Such a trend, however, has disturbing possibilities for the future. This coupled with the active hostility of some Harijans to the Hindu form of worship, as had been reported from certain places in Gujarat, are straws in the wind which it would be unwise to ignore. The conversion of Harijans to Islam in large numbers at Meenakshipuram in Tamil Nadu in the recent past, and the allegations of using Gulf money for this purpose, are all factor which though yet very minor, hold possibilities for a realignment of forces which is likely to generate reactive communalism in the majority community. It is this that is of concern for the purposes of the present study.

According to a report, Indian Muslims have been promised support by the World Islamic Fundamentalist Youth Movement for their struggle to uphold their Personal Law and their striving for "Political, social and economic justice". Recently, the World Assembly of Muslim Youth **(WAMY)** met at Riyadh for six days during which 53 papers including one on Indian Muslims were discussed.

These point to a process not of integration but of divisiveness between communities which just cannot be wished away. They are facts of life and they need to be faced squarely.

As long as politicians whether of the majority or the minority communities use the ignorant, illiterate and the fanatical fringe of the respective communities as their tools, communalism in the way in which it has played havoc with the lives and properties of people can never be eliminated from Indian society. The tendency to treat the communities as vote banks by the communal leaders, to win elections and perpetuate their leadership is one of the important causes of the growth of communalism over the years. When politics gets communalised, the political genius of a communalist consists in extracting the last ounce of political advantage even from the ruins of the people, regardless of whether they belong to the majority or the minority communities.

The concept of secular politics has received generally only lip service from many of the national political parties. What our politicians overlook or are not bothered about is the necessity for a composite and strong state structure responsible enough for dealing with the problems of a complex and plural society. If we are going to countenance communalism because it pays electoral dividends, we should not regret it if the communalism so promoted takes away also from the electoral gains. It is consistency and commitment to fundamentals of secularism rather than slogan-mongering and group-singing that will eliminate communalism. Instead of using the elections as occasions for building more bridges between the majority and minority communities and also between the different caste groups, political manoeuvring at the time of elections is destroying whatever bridges are still left between the communities.

The Raghubir Dayal Commission on the Ranchi-Hatia riots in 1967 observed: "The political parties should change their attitude in approaching the people for their gain. especially at elections. They should not exploit communal and caste feelings for their purposes. No political, economic or cultural issues should be discussed or agitated from a purely communal angle. Communal harmony should be taken to be too sacred to be tampered with for mere political gain".

The Madon Commission (1970) set up by the Maharashtra government to look into the Bhiwandi riots of 1970 observed: "There are political parties and other organisations which do not restrict their membership only to persons of a particular community. Nonetheless, their activities are communal and oriented to members of one community only. As a facade, they take a few persons of their communities as members and very often as office-bearers. There are office-seekers in every community and such persons can always be found to serve as a front in an attempt to cloak the real nature of such political party or organisation. Such parties and organisations in a state must be treated as communal organisations and communal bodies."

The three-member Commission set up in Bihar to inquire into the 1979 disturbances in and around Jamshedpur observed : "The list of recommendations will not be complete without a reference to the attitude of the political parties, in relation to matters connected with communalism. They have always regarded the communities as vote banks and directed their programmes and plan of action accordingly. Vote means power, and, to the politician's heart, power is dearer than any other considerations. This attitude must change. This is entirely a matter of political will and the Commission can do no more than invite attention to this malady and the imperative need of finding an appropriate remedy for it."

One of the imperatives of a plural society is the cultivation of an abiding faith between communities. This should enable the electoral representation of the interests of all by any candidate, regardless of the communal and caste denominations. Unfortunately however, this mutuality of faith which is the sine qua non of a secular society is not much in evidence. Addressing the 1961 September Conference on National Integration, Dr. Zakir Hussain(24) observed: "I am not sure of my facts, but Maulana Abul Kalam Azad was somebody in our national life. When he stood for election and a seat had to be found for him, it was found at Rampur because of the considerable Muslim votes there. But he refused to stand from Rampur. Then a seat was found at Gurgaon because of the considerable number of Meos there. But we should have put him up in a 100% Hindu constituency and got defeated. It might have been a defeat, but there would have been the moral victory of integration. The party might suffer, but then the party would come back with a stronger programme of integration". Such a happy state of affairs one can eventually hope to arrive at if only we take the first step forward in that direction. Presuming instead that the path to such a goal is packed with political mines and hence is not within the art of the possible in the prevailing political state of Indian politics, is to give up the fight even before it is begun. Fears imagined can be far more frightening than experiences lived through.

Only when political parties take a decision in principle that they will not exploit communalism as an expedient to win elections, either by setting up candidates belonging to only 'those communities who constitute a significant segment of the electorate in the concerned constituencies or who indulge in promises during the election campaign which have a distinct communal flavour, would we have taken the first and the most important step towards decommunalising politics and thereby giving the required support to secularism. It may be a worthwhile move towards bringing secularism to the grass roots if important national political parties can, as a matter of policy, avoid putting up candidates who belong to the same community as the largest number of voters in any constituency. This certainly has its limitations in terms of practical application. The conscious effort that has characterised the selection of candidates in the past has been to field minority candidates in constituencies which have a preponderance of the minority population. Such calculated aggravation of communalism can and should be abandoned as a matter of principle unless such a course has to be taken in any particular situation for reasons of transparent validity. May be that such a course will inevitably result in the loss of a few seats. But once all the national political parties adhere to this principle consistently the message will not fail to reach and be endorsed in due course by the people generally. As of now the tendency on the part of the national political parties to take an opportunistic stand towards communalism provides the much needed legitimacy to communal ideology and what is worse disables these political parties from making any positive move towards secularisation of politics.

IV

Case Studies of Communal Riots in Moradabad (1980), Bhiwandi (1984), Malegaon (1982), Biharsharif (1981), Belgaum (1984) and Ahmedabad (1985 and 1986)

Moradabad city in Uttar Pradesh has a Muslim population of 47%. After the riots in 1971, which were handled effectively, Moradabad had been free from communal tensions till August 19th 1980 when violence erupted again on Id-ul-Fitr day. The local residents put the figure of those killed between 250 and 300. The official figures were 144 persons killed. Most of the deaths occurred on the first day of the riots as a result of police firing. The incident was sparked off by the entry of a pig towards the Namazis (Muslims offering prayers) on the city side of the road. The Muslims thought that the police had been responsible for inducting the pig into the area and agitated crowds started throwing stones at the police. The Senior Superintendent of Police who was hit on the head collapsed and had to be removed. The Additional District Magistrate was dragged away by some six persons and was later found to have been done to death. The lynching of some of the policemen by the crowd led to heavy and indiscriminate firing at the crowd. The police outpost was surrounded, police arms looted and policemen beaten up. Three Constables were killed. The crowd then dispersed into the city and looting of shops started. The violence which initially started as a confrontation between the Muslims and the police soon turned into a communal riot between the Hindus and the Muslims. The breakdown of the administrative machinery during the first few days coupled with the spontaneous anger of the Muslim population against the police contributed considerably to the escalation of violence.

The Moradabad riot of 1980 was inquired into by Justice Saxena of the Allahabad High Court. He submitted his report in May, 1983. The report however has not been made public by the state government for whatever reason.

In connection with these riots 400 cases were registered under the Indian Penal Code, of which 125 were chargesheeted and 264 cases were closed after investigation for want of evidence. As on January 1986, II cases were still under investigation. 38 cases out of 125 which were put up in Court were withdrawn under the orders of the government. Of the remaining, 64 casės were acquitted and only 6 cases ended in conviction. These figures only reinforce the conclusion that something drastic needs to be done with regard to the registration, investigation and prosecution of cases arising out of the communal riots, if the authorities are to provide any deterrent against the recurrence of such diabolical riots. As things are, the police action in so far as it relates to the arrest and prosecution of persons involved in communal riots, has degenerated into a meaningless ritual. Why is it that so far we have not been able to take any corrective steps in this regard? Why does not an issue like this, which is very real and demands to be met squarely, figure on the agenda of the numerous National Integration Council meetings, considering the importance and impact it would have in similar riot cases? If the cause of the failure to come to grips with this problem in all its ramifications is to be laid at the door of the Criminal Justice System, what steps have we taken to correct this imbalance in the system even though prosecutions launched after every successive riot have met with no better result? These are very relevant questions to which the authorities have to address themselves, and find adequate and convincing answers. We will have occasion to reaffirm this conclusion when we examine the corresponding figures relating to the Bhiwandi riots of 1984.

The Brassware industry in Moradabad is largely controlled by the Hindus. They used to be the main exporters too till the 70s. The artisans however, are Muslims. In the recent past, Muslims have also taken to the export business. One of the sources of tension between Hindus and Muslims in Moradabad is due to the impression among Hindus that the Muslim exporters are favoured by the Muslim countries in the Gulf. This has created a certain amount of resentment among the Hindu businessmen. There are also allegations that the Muslims are over-invoicing the exports and are paid more than the legitimate prices of the articles. Funds for the various welfare and community activities of the Muslims are attributed to these sources from the Gulf. The newly acquired affluence among certain sections of the Muslims has given rise to the growth of a large number of religious and educational institutions in Lucknow, Moradabad and Varanasi. The Muslims have also been acquiring large properties particularly in the form of land, old houses, etc. In Varanasi it has reached a point where the Hindus who want to sell property would rather sell it at a slightly lower price to a non-Muslim than at a higher price to a Muslim. These are all the old possessions of ex-Bengali Zamindars from Bengal, who owned large houses along the Ganges at Varanasi.

In Bhiwandi in the State of Maharashtra, both Hindus and Muslims own powerloom factories. While the Hindu owners employ Muslim workers, Muslim owners also employ Hindu workers. The accounts of Muslim merchants are maintained by Hindu clerks. In the same building in Bhiwandi, there are both Hindu and Muslim powerloom owners. While the majority of the powerloom units are owned by Muslims, the supply of raw materials such as yarn and the disposal of the products in the markets are controlled by Hindu merchants. With such close inter-dependence between the two communities, one cannot easily believe that these very same people would be interested in disrupting the fabric of their daily lives. This only reinforces the conclusion that often it is the communal leaders who stand to gain something in the nature of personal, commercial or communal advantage, who promote such riots. Once a riot erupts, the mixed population which normally works together like brothers kills each other like sworn enemies. In the process, the only persons who gain are the communal fanatics.

Though Bhiwandi has a labour population of nearly three lakhs, there are no trade union activities among the labourers in Bhiwandi. This is not for want of trying by the trade union leaders. They had tried and failed largely because the employers had kept the labourers away from the influence of the trade union leaders on communal grounds. A calculated strategy of this type by the employers has kept them free from labour trouble though the advantage has been derived largely, if not entirely, on communal considerations. If there was healthy trade union activity in Bhiwandi, this may well have dissolved to a large extent the gang up on communal lines. The workers cutting across the communal divide would have come together on the basis of conditions of their service, wages, and the like. The exploitation by the vested interests of labour on communal lines while impoverishing them has accentuated the communal divide.

Bhiwandi is a classic example of how when a town grows in an unplanned manner but at a hectic pace, it can give rise to problems many of which manifest themselves in forms which are not related to the basic maladies and can find different manifestations.

There is a mass of floating population in Bhiwandi from different states which has converged on the town to work on daily wages. Their antecedents are not known to the local police. The manner in which they live, eat, and work should be a subject of study by itself. The place continues to bristle with activities most of which are highly irregular or illegal. Labour laws are indifferently enforced. This city is proliferating with problems and even if the authorities had been aware of them they had shown themselves until 1985 to be impervious. Several of these factors have contributed insidiously to the communal flare-ups that have been erupting periodically. Take a simple subject such as the registration of the looms. Out of about two and a half lakh looms, at least 40% were reportedly not registered. This leads to large-scale evasion of excise dues. Most of the electric connections are diverted and stolen. The electric wires hang loosely around because they are temporary, improvised, and unauthorised. In their anxiety to make quick money, the concerned authorities are callous to the dangers of short-circuit of naked wires.

In places liked Bhiwandi, Moradabad and Aligarh conditions conducive to the build-up of tension are created everyday by several factors many of which have nothing to do with communalism as such. These have relevance to the several civic and administrative matters in the towns. Failure to handle them appropriately and effectively and in the context of the expectations of modern living create conditions in which over-crowding, frustrations and anger give rise to tensions which eventually manifested as communal riots. If an attempt is made to understand the various aspects of life in these towns, each of which while seemingly unrelated to the communal ethos, cumulatively creates conditions in which periodically large-scale violence is facilitated.

In Bhiwandi most of the people can be seen defecating on the narrow roads or whatever other open places they can find. They can be seen eating in hundreds in the local eating houses known as 'Bhisis' where they squat and eat their daily food. Since there is no place for many of them to rest, they take their turn to sleep inside small cubicles, where dozens of people live and sleep while the others work on looms. The level of the basic civic amenities such as sanitation, drainage, drinking water and health-care, is a matter of utter shame. The Municipality should have been long upgraded to the level of a Corporation with a senior officer capable of taking important decisions on the spot. The Municipality had only two outdated fire tenders at the time of the riot in 1984. There is no Municipal hospital at Bhiwandi. The result has been that serious injuries in normal times and more so during riots have to be treated in Thane which is about 25 kilometres from Bhiwandi.

The total strength of the town police officers and men in Bhiwandi in 1984 was about 250 distributed over three Police Stations. One company (99 men) of Special Reserve Police was attached to Bhiwandi, Thane and Kalyan after the 1970 riots. At the time of the 1970 riots in Bhiwandi there was only one Police Station which was increased to three after the riots. As a result of the 1984 riots there has been an increase by about 300 men as against the Police Department's estimated requirement of about 800 men. Many of the police personnel stay in the slums of Bhiwandi for want of official quarters. In the process, the possibility of the police personnel absorbing a part of the slum culture cannot be ruled out. The effect that this would have when they are called upon to handle riots when these occur is not difficult to imagine.

An exercise has since been started in Bhiwandi town planning in the later half of 1985 presumably as a sequel to the toll of 174 lives in the communal riots of 1984.

Following the riot in Bhiwandi on 18th May 1984, riots erupted in more than a dozen places in Bombay soon after the night prayers of the Muslims. 89 persons lost their lives in the Bombay riots, of which 49 died in police firing. Among the dead were one Sub-Inspector and one Head Constable. Two other policemen received gun shot injuries due to firing by the mob on May 18th night and three others on 19th afternoon.

The Centre for Research in Rural and Industrial Development, Chandigarh did a study in August, 1985 of the communal violence in Bhiwandi in 1984 and Pune in 1982 and its impact on development and national integration.

According to this study, a majority of powerloom workers, who happen to be Hindus in certain areas of Bhiwandi complained about the lack of health care, education, sanitation and drinking water facilities in their localities. These workers considered the neglect of their localities to be an issue designed by the majority of the Muslims who dominated the Municiplity, to make life miserable for the Hindu minority. The merchant manufactuers who happen to be Ansari Muslims, residing in certain areas of Bhiwandi complained that Hindu traders delayed payment for cloth that they sold to them and deducted illegitimate 'Kardhas' or discounts as they are a helpless Muslim minority in India. These merchants wanted a new cloth market to be constructed in Bhiwandi and felt that only such a market could save the Muslims from Hindus. This demand for a new cloth market is opposed by the Hindus, as according to them, such a market in Bhiwandi will sound the death-knell of Hindu control over the cloth trade.

According to the survey, the 1984 riots were largely the outcome of business rivalry, though the immediate provocation was provided by the Shivaji Jayanthi procession. The well-entrenched and the newly emerging traders came to perceive competition between them in trade along religious lines. When the competition happens to be between merchants belonging to two religious groups, communal motives are imputed for the success or the failure of the different groups. During the riots of 1965 and 1982 in Pune and 1970 in Bhiwandi it was the anti-social elements who provoked the riots. In the subsequent stages of the 1984 riots in Bhiwandi a section of builders used anti-social elements to get vacated their lands where powerloom workers had constructed jhuggis converting their properties into slums. Some of the loom owners incidently also developed a vested interest in prolonging the communal riots so that they could buy looted beams of yarn from the anti-social elements. This also enhanced the duration and intensity of the riots. Some of these examples give one the impression that riots are becoming economic goal oriented.

Malegaon in Maharashtra had witnessed communal riots in November 1982, and June 1983. The earlier one was provoked by a controversy over the alleged disparaging reference about the Prophet in an 8th standard Marathi text book. The Muslims were agitated over the word 'Palayan (flight) used with reference to the Prophet. The June 1983 riots were sparked off by explosion of crackers outside a Masjid on 26th June, a day after the Indian Cricket team's victory in the Prudential World Cup Tournament. This was one of the worst riots and it lasted till 30th June. In all, four persons were killed and about 30 injured in Police firing. Malegaon has several characteristics which in combination make a town riot-prone. It has 67.5% Muslim population. The Muslims in Malegaon are generally prosperous businessmen. Of the 150 big powerlooms and sizing units, 147 belong to the Muslims and only 3 are owned by the Hindus. Malegaon has an Islamic seminary and is considered an important centre of Islamic learning. It has a number of Muslim weavers, who because of their poverty, depend for credit on the Hindu money lenders. Malegaon is yet another example of how the vested interests of businessmen combine to exploit the communal divide. The elites of both the communities do not let the workers avail of the Trade Union activities, by appealing to their communal feelings. While the Muslim powerloom owners thus have managed to keep the workers' wages down, the Hindu traders who have a monopoly of trade in the finished products of the looms get the products cheaper thereby making profits.

In the communal riots of Biharsharif in Bihar which took place on 30th April 1981 and the following days, according to the government figures the number of killed was 47 persons and that of the injured 68. The riot enveloped the rural areas and took a heavy toll of life and property during the next four days. The immediate cause of the communal riot in Biharsharif was a dispute between the Muslims and the Yadavs over a piece of land which was being used by the Muslims as a cemetery. Asghar Ali Engineer who had done a field study of the Biharsharif riots came to the conclusion that this riot was organised by those who wanted to stop the upward social mobility of the Scheduled Castes and the Muslims, as they did not want these deprived communities. to get any share of the fruits of development. To the extent that this problem has been examined, this theory has only a broad relevance and is çertainly not a factor in promoting communal riot in different places. A theory of this nature is more easily stated than convincingly proved by facts and figures. The victims of these riots were not businessmen who had established themselves or were in the process of doing so, but those at the bottom of the socio-economic ladder who had to depend on their daily wages for their survival. It would be nearer the truth to say that the vested interests among the communal elements from both the communities look out for an occasion to trigger off a riot, more with a view to feed the cancerous communal ideology among the ignorant and vulnerable members of their respective communities for its own sake, which in turn produces the bitterness between the communities which is exploited to divide them. This tends to give the more insecure among the groups an identity which otherwise tends to be amorphous at that level because of the ruthless mechanics of earning a living to feed hungry mouths. As far as the communal elements who promote the riots are concerned, to them the victims serve a communal purpose. Having served the purpose, they are quietly forgotten. In the process the usual fuss is made about the relief and rehabititation of the faimly members of the victims. One wonders how many of the families of the victims, be it in Aligarh, Moradabad, Bhiwandi, Biharsharif or Bombay, have been visited by the communal leaders of the two communities, once the fuss and publicity has died down.

The communal riot that broke out in Belgaum in Karnataka on 5th October, 1984 was the culmination of a controversy over the naming of a particular square in the market. The Muslims had been referring to it as the Jinnah chowk and the Hindus wanted it named as Veer Savarkar Chowk. At one of the meetings convened by the Divisional Commissioner, both the groups agreed to name it as Maulana Azad Chowk. But this suggestion was turned down by the government on the ground that the naming of streets, squares and similar things should be taken up only after the local bodies were constituted. The tension continued to build up. On 5th October, 1984 a Muslim of unsound mind desecrated a Hindu temple and this provided the spark in an atmosphere which was already charged. Very provocative slogans had been raised by the Hindus and writings in Kannada and Marathi newspapers had been highly communal and vituperative before the 5th of October. In the riots that followed, several shops were looted and then set on fire. The rioting continued for five days. If only the authorities had sorted out the issue of renaming the square which had been agitating the people from 1982, this ugly riot could have been prevented. This was inspite of the fact that a front organisation of the Hindu Sabha named Hindu Ekta Andolan had been agitating over the years on this issue on blatantly communal lines. Even then no preventive action was taken by the police against the leaders, nor were the printers and publishers of provocative articles in papers proceeded against. On the basis of the study, it can be safely asserted that the local police were not effective enough to mobilise the available force and deal with the situation competently.

The anti-reservation agitation of 1985 in Ahmedabad which converted itself into a prolonged communal riot holds several important lessons for the authorities, if only they are prepared to benefit from them. Why did the communal riots continue over a period of months in 1985, albeit sporadically with very brief periods of tenuous peace? It is not in the nature of communal riots to fester as they did in Ahmedabad. In Independent India there have been riots of great intensity and virulence between the communities, involving large areas and with very severe loss of life and property. But then these riots had generally been of the type which normally did not last beyond a week or ten days at the most, followed by periods of tension and bitterness. Later, the tension had generally drained off over a period of time by the induction of extra force wherever necessary and by the activities of the authorities and the voluntary organisations, which often had a very helpful and purposeful hand in restoring peace and amity between the communities.

If there is one area in which the police has to and must act firmly and decisively right from the beginning, it is in the handling of communal riots. By doing so it would be kind to both the communities. Such handling alone can save innocent lives and avert avoidable damage to property. The lesson that ought to be driven home by such firmness to the anti-social and fanatical elements, who are the first to be on the scene is that the authorities will not tolerate communal rioting whatever be the cost. This is also the most opportune time to take into the police net, dead or alive, as many of the anti-social elements and fanatics who promote and profit from such carnages. These elements, given time, will soon disappear into the sanctuaries from where they will continue to stoke the communal fire. Once the rioters get the initial impression that the authorities are weak or indecisive in the use of force, the riot spreads fast and wide, taking in its wake avoidable loss in terms of innocent lives and property. This is exactly the message that went down in Ahmedabad in 1985, whether it was intended or not.

One of the recent trends in communal riots is the motivation of communal elements who engineer the riots with a view to making what are presently mixed localities into homogeneous ones. Apart from the security aspect implied in this move, there is also an economic angle. They expect the minorities in the respective pockets to make distress sale of their properties at throw-away prices in their anxiety to move to areas in which the majority of their community live. During the Ahmedabad communal riots of 1985 it was alleged that there was a deep seated political-police-underworld nexus, which was interested in such sales. The government responded to this very effectively by refusing to recognise the transactions relating to the transfer of property which had taken place after a particular date.

In the first week of January, 1986 Ahmedabad had yet one more communal riot. Though the riot had its origin in a quarrel between two families over some children who ran across terraces while flying kites, this led to a pitched battle between the two communities. Whatever may have been the immediate provocation, the real cause of the riot seems to have been provided by the supporters of the mafia leader, Alamzeb, who was killed earlier at Surat. According to police sources the mafia leader used to finance the communal elements and had supplied them with arms. The Muslims of Ahmedabad in certain areas also observed a 'Bandh' when the news of Alamzeb's death was received.

The 1982 Baroda riots had much to do with rivalry between Hindu and Muslim criminal gangs over the control of the illicit liquor trade.

There was police firing in the Aligarh Muslim University campus on May 12, 1981. Asghar Ali Engineer was one of the members of the fact-finding team which visited Aligarh in the month of August, 1981. This was sponsored by the Citizens for Democracy. Asghar Ali Engineer has observed(25): "Extreme poverty, miserable living conditions, inhuman exploitation of child labour in the household lock manufacturing industry are some of the characteristics of Aligarh. There are reported to be 40,000 children working for a pittance of Re.1/- a day in Aligarh." The hostel accommodation in Aligarh Muslim University campus is woefully short. While the total accommodation available is far less than 4,000 seats, not less than 9,000 students are residing in the hostels. Thus overcrowding has led to certain serious problems. The authorities do not have a proper record of accommodation. Many students do not pay for the hostel accommodation and quite often bad characters live in hostels. It is obvious that most of the teachers accept the fact of corruption and malfunctioning of the University. Even the Students Union President had issued a statement which focussed on corruption in the University. In an interview published in the Urdu magazine, 'Khair-O-Khabar' in its April, 1980 issue, the Union President had complained that the Aligarh Muslim University degrees had been devalued and approvingly quoted a teacher who had told him: "If I were an employer, I would not have employed these boys because they have not read anything". According to the student leader, "Some criminal elements want to destroy the peace in our alma mater. Incompetent administration.... unwillingness to take steps against criminal elements and lack of moral courage on the part of the University administration" were some of the factors responsible for the sad state of affairs in the University campus.

This atmosphere contributes no less to creating conditions in which communalism thrives.

A remarkable feature of communal riots in general is the insignificant beginning that most of these riots usually have. Very often it is a criminal act indulged in by an individual or two belonging to one particular community which is objected to or resented by an individual or two of another community. Such an incident which is basically criminal in nature normally does not find supporters and godfathers if it is against the members of the same community. But the communal virus has gone so deep into our system that it comes alive in its ugliest and cruelest manifestations if the other party to the incident belongs to a different community. In such an event, even a private quarrel gets vested with communal trappings.

Some of the common causes which trigger off communal riots have been:

1) Encroachment on places of worship
2) Disputes over land belonging to places of worship;
3) Music before mosques;
4) Teasing of girls belonging to the other community;
5) Desecration of places of worship;
6) Petty quarrels between members belonging to different communities;
7) Conversion; and
8) Provocative articles in magazines.

Though these causes provide the immediate provocations, it would not be right to conclude that they alone are the causes. It would be more realistic to state that these are the catalysts which galvanize into riots an atmosphere which is permeated with the posion of communalism. The creation of this atmosphere and the perception of the members belonging to the two communities about each other have all to be viewed in the context of the several factors which have all been referred to as contributing to communalism in the first part of this study. The immediate causes which triggered off the riots would not have been the catalysts that they turned out to be, unless the soil had been prepared over months and years and was ready for the first and even the flimsiest provocations to explode into a riot.

Rumour plays a leading and mischievous role in fanning the flames in a surcharged atmosphere. What is worse, lately affluent people belonging to different communities participate in the riots, albeit from behind the scenes, by financing the members of their respective communities for the purchase of fire arms or even actually supplying them with firearms. This happened in the Bombay and Bhiwandi riots when one of the known and notorious criminals was found responsible for supplying money and arms to his followers to participate in the riots.

There is a mistaken belief that a riot can be dealt with and disposed off in isolation. Anyone who has handled a communal situation and worked through the incidents erupting, developing and proliferating would know that the authorities are called upon to handle not merely individuals or groups who are bent upon looting, burning and killing each other, but communities of people who are fired by intense anger and hatred, wanting to do the worst they can against members of the other community, regardless of whether or not the victims share the responsibility in creating the situation. Reason deserts and the only prevailing human emotions are of anger and revenge. These emotions get further aggravated by the mixed composition of the population in certain cities like Bhiwandi, Ahmedabad, Delhi and other places. Many of those who theorise about the preventing and handling of communal riots fail to take account of the fact that in the type of geographical locations that the two communities live and work, it requires exceptional goodwill, understanding and harmony to be able to live in peace specially during periods of tension. Under the prevailing conditions of over crowding, insanitation and all the ills that go with these even brothers tend to fly at each other's throats. To expect under these circumstances, that communities whose communal feelings have been stirred up by certain individuals and organisations, month after month and over the years, would live in peace, is indeed unrealistic. Even so, let it be said to their credit and to the shame of their leaders that by and large they have learnt to live and let live, and have established a sort of working relation and amity which holds generally, unless and until it is distrupted by forces which seek to exploit the inherent and built-in differences for petty, communal, political and occasionally competitive commercial interests.

A Police officer who was incharge of the Gujarat Police Computer in 1985 and who did an analysis with the help of the computer of a few of the communal riots which had occurred in Gujarat, came up with certain interesting findings. some of these are:

1) Invariably the weapons used during the riots are of the type which are found in any ordinary household such as razors, knives, guptis, etc.

This however, is fast changing. More explosive and sophisticated fire arms have been in evidence in some of the recent riots elsewhere in the country. Even in the Ahmedabd riots of 1985, the police was able to recover considerable quantities of incendiary material, detonators, gelatine rods and high explosive bombs. These were being supplied from outstations to the rioters at Ahmedabad. Use of high-level firepower and explosives has become a feature of recent communal riots.

2) The incidents get concentrated in certain areas where the communal elements have an extra degree of aggressiveness. In the majority of incidents the victims belong to the same area. It

is only in a small percentage of cases that the victims belong to different localities. The victims in such cases many have strayed into the areas for certain compulsory chores without realising the risks to which they were exposing themselves.

This finding has important relevance in establishing that if an area is taken charge of by a unit of the police force and dealt with intensely and systematically by way of patrolling and supervision, it is possible to contain and smother the trouble at the start of the situation and prevent it from becoming serious.

3) Another of the findings was that in most of these incidents the initiative was taken by mobs though there were incidents of violence for which individuals or groups of two or three were responsible.

4) The study also showed that among the arrested, there were a large number of persons with previous criminal records.

This should be interpreted more as an indication of the tendency on the part of the police on all such occasions to go for the known criminals. It is very difficult to get to know the real culprits because of the several factors which help the miscreants to act anonymously. The fact that a large number of communal riot cases get acquitted in courts is entirely because of the very factors which contribute to their anonymity. This is however, not to deny the inevitable gangups that are common on such occasions. One group may give the names of the rival miscreants but then to process a case through the courts on the basis of evidence tendered by such witnesses has its own constraints. As happened in the case of the Bhiwandi riots of 1984, with regard to more than 30 odd persons who were prosecuted for the massacre of 21 persons on the spot in the course of one incident at Ansaribagh, the judge came to the conclusion that there was no independent and corroborative evidence against any of the accused and discharged all of them. Even with regard to the persons present, the judge came to the conclusion that this fact could be established with regard to only three or four of the accused. The Judge said in his oral judgement at the end of the two-month long trial that the prosecution did not utter a single word against 30 of the 40 accused, let alone involve them in the crime. The Madon Commission which inquired into the 1970 communal riots in Bhiwandi. Malad and Jalgaon in Maharashtra observed: "that the Special Investigation Squads set up to investigate the crimes committed in the course of this riot had acted in a baised manner against one community". The Police Commission which had looked into the reports of some of these riots felt that there were many instances wherein the Special Investigation Squads were not set up properly, with the result that some of them had acted in an incompetent and partisan manner.

The fact remains that it is very difficult to get to know the real offenders who commit these crimes unless they are caught on the spot by independent witnesses or by the authorities themselves. This is a very rare phenomenon. the result inevitably is that communal riot cases seldom end in conviction and therefore, the criminal proceedings following the riots have seldom acted as a deterrent in the prevention and handling of subsequent communal riots. In this connection, the statement given in Table 11 about the registered cases arising out of the Bhiwandi riots of 1984 and their disposal should set at rest doubts, if any, about the utter futility of all the police efforts that follow during and after the riots by way of arrests, investigations and prosecutions of those alleged to have participated in the riots. Out of the 611 cases registered, only 185 cases i.e. 30.8 per cent of the cases were sent up to the court in May/June 1984. Of these, as many as 113 cases i.e. 61 per cent were acquitted, and only four cases, **repeat only four cases,** had ended in conviction by January, 1986 i.e. after a lapse of eighteen months. Sixtyfive cases were still pending. They are not likely to fare any better. That this should have been the result in a state like Maharashtra where the administration generally and police administration in particular still enjoy a degree of reputation for effectiveness and purposefulness, is a matter for concern.

Table 11

Statement Showing the Disposal of cases Reported in the Month of May 1984 (Bhiwandi Riot) Thane Commissionerate (Upto January 1986)

Sr. No.	Police Station	Reported	Accused Arrested	Cases sent up	Convicted	Acquitted	Compounded	*Pending Trial*	Final Report
1	2	3	4	5	6	7	8	9	10
1.	Turbhe	9	8	3	—	2	—	1	6
2.	Rabale	26	103	20	—	19	—	1	6
3.	Thanenagar	73	62	13	—	4	—	9	60
4.	Naupada	115	80	8	—	3	3	2	107
5.	Wagale Estate	61	389	39	1	18	—	20	22
6.	Vartaknagar	53	184	20	—	16	—	4	33
7.	Kapurbawadi	77	71	15	—	9	—	6	62
8.	Bhiwandi	61	159	19	1	18	—	—	42
9.	Nizampura	44	318	16	1	9	—	6	28
10.	Bhoiwada	63	537	15	1	7	—	7	48
11.	M.F.C. Kalyan	12	20	7	—	5	—	2	5
12.	Bazarpeth	17	226	10	—	3	—	7	7
	Total	611	2157	185	4	113	3	65	426

This should prove conclusively that criminal prosecution of the miscreants for their acts during the riots is not deterrent and effective enough to prevent them from participating in subsequent riots. On the contrary, for a gang of criminals including those who promote and indulge in communal riots, every unpunished crime and act of violence is a precedent, a full dress rehearsal for more vicious and violent crime. In view of the communal and criminal elements participating in the riots, it is necessary to employ modern techniques of video recording and other sophisticated photographic aids to register as much of the actual riot as possible so that the same could be used later on in evidence. This would require that the cities and towns which are prone to communal riots are equipped with fullly protected and secured mobile vans fitted with video recording facilities which should be capable of being used as evidence at the time of prosecution. If necessary, the law will also have to be amended to make evidence of this type admissible. Unless some such special and concerted steps are taken it would not be possible to prosecute successfuly the communal elements and create in the process the deterrent effect required to prevent recurrence of such incidents. The discouraging results of the prosecution of communal riot cases in the past would amply justify recourse to such new methods if legal action is to have a deterrent effect not only on the anti-social elements but also on some of the communal leaders, who occasionally make brief appearances on all such occasions to incite their communal followers. During the 1985 Shivaji Jayanti procession in Bhiwandi, the district authorities had covered the procession with television cameras, which according to the Chief Secretary of the state, enabled a very close coverage of the participants. This also had a deterrent effect on the mischievous elements.

If therefore, a communal riot is to cease to become a source of investment for communal vested interests steps will have to be taken to provide all the cities and towns which are notoriously riot prone with these modern techniques of covering occasions which have the potential of communal trouble.

V

Commissions of Inquiry

Writing editorially on the Biharsharif communal riots in 1981 'MAINSTREAM' (26) observed: "As usual the state government was slow in reacting to the first outbreak and then the attempt was to cover up the failure of the administration by playing down the seriousness of what had happened." The problem with our handling of communal riots is that more often than not the district authorities fail to act promptly and effectively in dealing with a communal situation. What is still worse is their tendency to suppress and conceal the facts in the mistaken belief that in doing so they are saving the prestige of the government. This has had two consequences: One is that there is allround anxiety and effort not to let facts be known to people who matter outside the districts even within the state. The second consequence is that having concealed the hardcore facts and given a version which is totally or even partially divorced from the realities of the situation, everything that follows in the form of judicial or administrative inquiries is influenced, if not calculated towards sustaining the theories initially set out at a responsible level of the government. In the manipulation which is sometimes involved, even total change of records has not been unknown.

Inquiry commissions have necessarily to base their conclusions on the basis of the evidence presented before them. They cannot go behind the evidence. If the evidence is based on distortions of facts and documents, to that extent conclusions are also likely to be affected. It is difficult to assert that the evidence presented before the commissions inquiring into communal riots is always based on the factual position and has not been doctored.

"Wherever a judicial inquiry is decided upon, it is necessary, if that inquriy is to serve an useful purpose, that all evidence in favour and against the authorities be unreservedly placed before the commission of inquiry by the government itself and that government should adopt not a partisan attitude before the Commission. We have elsewhere pointed out the handicaps which this Commission was faced with in this regard."(27)

The implications of these observations made by Justice Jaganmohan Reddy Commission which looked into the 1969 riots in Ahmedabad and other places in Gujarat are quite clear. It is one thing for the people involved in the riots to have escaped the killing. It is quite another to escape the memory of it. Very often the facts and documents brought before the Commission about the riots are not on the basis of how exactly the riot took place but what the parties including the officials would have liked the facts to be. The perishability of facts concerning communal riots is not as obvious to the members of the public as it is to the officials who handle the riots or even to those members of the public who participate in the riots. Inevitably truth is one of the important casualties in the findings arrived at by the Commissions on the basis of the distorted facts presented before them.

Why cannot a concerted and coordinated study be done in peace time about the alleged constribution of the **R.S.S.** to the Biharsharif riots, the happenings in the Aligarh University campus where the cry "Islam in danger" was raised by interested groups, the economic rivalry that promoted the riots in Bhiwandi and in Moradabad? Unless such a study is done by a set of people drawn from different regions and disciplines and firm conclusions arrived at, it will not be possible to deal with the communal problem intelligently and pragmatically. Instead of this what actually happens is that, every riot brings in its wake the usual editorials in the national dailies deploring the incidents; the same political and communal leaders descend on the scene and issue the same type of statements making allegations against the rival political and communal parties. Occasionally an inquiry Commission looks into the peripheral aspects of the riots and comes up with a report months or even years later when the subject may well have moved out of the people's minds. The Madon Commission(28) which looked into the Bhiwandi riots of 1970 took more than three years to submit its report. Very often the appointment of an Inquiry Commission has been motivated by considerations of administrative or political expediency, to tide over the pressures of the demand for such an inquiry from the leaders of the opposition political parties and community leaders. Thereafter one can trust the Commission to cool the issue completely by the amount of time it takes to eventually submit its report. Seldom has the report of an Inquiry Commission been read, commented and acted upon with the same anxiety that marked the demand for the appointment of it at the level of the people and the leaders who originally demanded it, or for that matter even at the level of the government.

The Aligarh Riots Commission headed by Justice Shashi Kant Varma was appointed on October 20, 1978. It was wound up on July 31, 1980. This was how the position was explained in reply to a question in the Rajya Sabha: "The Commission was required to submit its report within four months. However, its term was extended piece-meal, from time to time, till at last the Commission came up with a request in April 1980 for a further extension of its term by at least one and a half years to enable it to complete the inquiry.

While the Commission had to examine more than 200 witnesses, for a variety of reasons, it examined only eight from the date of appointment in January 21, 1980. In view of this slow progress of inquiry, as also the state government's assessment that the continuance of the inquiry Commission might generate additional tensions, the state government ordered the winding up of this Commission with effect from July 31st, 1980 under the relevant provisions of the Commissions of Inquiry

Act. The winding up of the Commission by the state government was not based on any advice given by the Central government."

The latest example of casualness and lack of purpose that characterises the appointment of Commissions of Inquiry is the appointment of the Desai Commission by the Gujarat government in June, 1986 to inquire into the riots that ravaged Ahmedabad in 1985. It took the Gujarat administration about a year to appoint the Commission. Whether such a belated appointment serves any political purpose or not, one has serious doubts about its function and usefulness in diagnosing and resolving the communal problem that afflicted Ahmedabad in 1985.

Experiences such as these with the Commissions of Inquiry into communal riots should set us thinking on the very utility of such inquiries and their relevance to the understanding of the problem of communal violence and in ascertaining the steps that can help in eradicating it. It is worth considering to what extent the recommendations of such Commissions have been followed up and implemented in the past. It may also be useful to examine whether in the light of our past experiences with the working of the Commissions, and the lack of interest if not actual indifference in the matter of implementation of their several recommendations, a fresh, more practical and expeditious approach to ascertaining the truth behind communal and other forms of violence and the immediate practical steps that can be taken to prevent the recurrence of such violence, should be thought of. One must accept the fact that plumbing the depths of the communal malady and analysing its several pathological components is administratively and investigationally an intricate affair, which may also be politically inconvenient and even inexpedient. An elaborate and exhaustive inquiry almost on the lines of the Presidential Commission of America which went into the ethnic riots in the United States in 1967 will need to be undertaken to cover the entire gamut of the problem in the cities and towns which have become prone to communal violence in recent years.

Ranchi-Hatia riots of August, 1967(29) were inquired into by a Commission consisting of three members under the Chairmanship of Justice Raghubir Dayal. Some of the findings of this Commission when viewed in the light of the subsequent events would prove that regardless of what the Commissions say in their reports, the same mistakes continute to be repeated, be it with regard to the measures to be taken to avert a communal riot or with regard to controlling it in quick time. The Raghubir Dayal Commission had pointed out that "directions or interference from the highest level in government not only restricts the local officers from taking independent decisions on the problems confronting them but also deprives their superiors of their right to criticise the actions of the local officers if the results are not what they expected or the acts committed are not quite in conformity with the law"

According to the Commission in matters such as the arresting of students who were involved, the police had to await instructions from the government. "The episode does not do credit to the government or its policy with regard to the action to be taken against the students".

Even as far back as 1967 the conflict between the police and the Army units inducted in aid of civil power had been evident. The Commission observed: "not only confusion but some sort of resentment arose in the police against their being placed under military as would appear from their referring people to the military when they approached them for certain help.... It is clear that the coordination and cooperation expected between the military and the police were probably not there."

The Commission had also put on record evidence to the effect that the "Police was simply watching and doing nothing." Both the District Magistrate and the Superintendent of Police were new to the district and hence were not in a position to appreciate the developing communal situation appropriately. They evidently did not know even the topography of the city and its vulnerable points. The intelligence system was 'admitedly not satisfactory'. It may be mentioned that in earlier years care was always taken not to change both the District Magistrate and Superintendent of Police at the same time.

Though one of the causes of the disturbances at Ranchi was attributed to the economic rivalry between the Muslims and the refugees from the Punjab, the Commission came to the conclusion: "We do not think that any such economic rivalry was responsible for the commencement of the riot, though this feeling could have been exploited once the disturbances started". Inadequate action by the police to deal with the anti-socials has been brought out very emphatically in the report. "It seems that after some tussle and clashes in the underworld, the Muslim and Hindu goondas divided the towns between themselves and a code was evolved wherein one was not to operate in the area of the other".

Many of the findings cited above from the Raghubir Dayal Commission, which submitted its report in 1968, could appropriately be transposed into the findings of the inquiry Commission, appointed in June, 1986 to look into the Ahmedabad riots of 1985.

The Jagmohan Reddy Commission which went into the riots in Ahmedabad and other towns in Gujarat on and after 18th September, 1969 had pointed out that there was lack of firmness on the part of the police in the initial stages when incidents were happening. "Police lost the initiative and once the situation got out of control at the very commencement of the riot, they were overwhelmed by the situation which confronted them". No wonder this riot took such a heavy toll of human lives. The official figures of those killed in Ahmedabad reported by the Commission stood at 524.

The Commission observed that the "evidence of the Army Officers showed what amount of confusion existed when they took over, how the mobs showed scant respect for the Police, and how it took time for them to create an impression upon the groups that they were not Police but the Army."

The three-member Judicial Inquiry Commission under the chairmanship of Justice Jitendra Narayan (30) which looked into the Jamshedpur riots of 1979 had commented adversely on the failure of the administration to comprehend the gravity of the situation preceding the riots and failing to take adequate steps. A leaflet which had been issued by an organisation called "Kendriya Akhada Samity', was highly provocative. It carried the message that: "a survey had established that all Policemen, Havildars, Home Guards, etc. were at heart ready to give support to them", in the procession that they intended to take out on the occasion of the Ram-navami Puja. The Commission commented: "Such was the failure of the District Administration to assess the dangerous portents of this leaflet in circulation that in a meeting which was held in the afternoon of April 9, 1979 in which the Commissioner took stock of the situation, this matter was not even brought up before him."

Regarding the police firing and the casualties, the Commission observed: "Allegations have been made that the Bihar Military Police fired recklessly and killed Muslims in their homes.... According to evidence on record, it appears that as many as 100 rounds were fired by the Police within a short time. After all this firing, which was supposed to be aimed at Muslim mobs.... two Muslims were found dead with bullet wounds, one inside a house and another in a lavatory. The Commission has no hesitation in observing that a noticeable link is discernible between claims made in the leaflet referred to above and the conduct exhibited by the Bihar Military Police sepoys."

One of the senior Army Officers whose units had been called out for controlling the Jamshedpur riots mentioned to me that when the Army came on the scene, almost within three hours after the outbreak of the riots, there was not much riot police in evidence on the streets. There is no reason to disbelieve the statement. This falls in line with the contents of the leaflet and the sympathies that the police units at the subordinate level were alleged to have evinced towards the organisers of the Hindu religious procession.

All the findings of the different Commissions pointed to, among others, certain serious flaws in the administrative system of the state concerned. But seldom were these attended to as a part of the follow-up actions which should in fact be treated as integral to the inquiry itself. It is such indifference if not apathy to curing the system that leads one to the conclusion that each of the commissions of inquiry having met the immediate purpose of defusing an inconvenient political situation, had fulfilled itself and mattered no more.

VI

Role of the Army and the Para Military Units in Communal Situations

It is necessary to understand that in civil disturbances the Army cannot always be effective without prejudice to its prestige. By inducting the Army to deal with disorder, the authorities acknowledge an elevation in the 'combat status' of the capability of the forces which manipulate and engineer civil disorders. No one is better suited and placed to understand this manipulation and deal with it effectively than the police who are expected to know the sober elements among the population as also the anti-social ones. The absence of proper understanding between the police and the army commands can give rise to complications, which in turn can render both the force ineffective. In a sense this is what happened in Ahmedabad. The helplessness and the ineffectiveness of the Army was shown up in dealing with the civil disorder when among other things, the women belonging to both the communities came out in very large numbers in different situations and rendered the Army ineffective. The Army could have got on top of the situation only by resorting to firing. Shooting was obviously not the answer for dealing with abusive and defiant women. Once the ineffectiveness of the Army in certain situations was demonstrated, it became an invitation for the repetition of the same strategy by the rioters, followed by the recurrence of violence.

The troops are trained not to retreat. If therefore in a civil disorder situation they do have to retreat or have to watch a situation helplessly, it is regarded as a sign of weakness which they cannot afford to display. Once the army is committed, it has to be successful. Any sign of failure or weakness would be psychologically disastrous both for the government and the people. It is therefore, imperative that the commitment of the army in a situation of civil disorder should be pushed as far back in time as possible by the induction of paramilitary forces and forces specially trained for handling communal and similar situations. Though the induction of the army in aid of civil power increases the state power in the short run, it exposes the inherent weakness of the state and renders the law and order institutions ineffective in the long run.

According to Major General Afsir Karim, who was commanding the army troops in the city of Ahmedabad, during the riots in 1985, "Peace could not return to Ahmedabad only because the anti-social elements were not being rounded up by the police". The depth of the communal virus should be evident from a question a delegation of Hindus put to an Army Officer. The Army Officer was shocked when he was asked as to why he had ordered firing on Hindu mobs when he himself was a Hindu. General Karim is reported to have remarked: "If caste and communal feelings get into the army, the greatest beneficiaries will be our enemies across the border."

The lack of understanding between the local police and the army units inducted in Ahmedabad during the riots, apart from being unfortunate and avoidable, also made serious inroads into the operational efficiency of both the army and the police units for want of mutual cooperation and coordination. Allegations and counter-allegations were made which became a matter of public knowledge through the Press. This had its own repercussions in the day-to-day relationship between the army and the police and in effect on their respective functioning. The rift was fully exploited by the anti-social elements with the inevitable loss in the effectiveness of the forces. It even seemed at one stage that the forces against law and order had triumphed though only briefly. The damage done to the reputation of the army and the police during that particular period was incalculable and out of proportion to the nature and extent of the differences between the security forces.

One can almost generalise in the light of our experience over the years that whenever the army is inducted in aid of civil power in communal situations, petty and avoidable differences between the army and the police have come in the way of the happy relationship and coordinated working of the two. This aspect has also been commented upon by some of the Commissions which have inquired into the riots in the past. That this lack of operational rapport should persist inspite of the several references to it by the different Commissions, is rather disturbing. To what extent does one attribute this continuing failure to conform to the ground rules that do exist and which lay down the guidelines governing the roles of both the army and the police in times of civil disorder? It is not that the problem is insoluble, but that, for whatever reason, we have not brought to bear on the issue the required resoluteness to resolve it once and for all. But every such failure is at the cost of the operational efficiency of the security forces which in turn detracts from the credibility and confidence that they are expected to inspire in the people of the land.

A similar thing happened on the occasion of the Moradabad riots in 1980 when the local police and the Border Security Force which was inducted in aid of the local authorities failed to cooperate and coordinate their respective operational responsibilities. The local police resented the suggestion of handing over the situation to the Border Security Force. The suggestion itself was construed as a reflection on their performance and competence. It needs to be spelt out clearly that the task of the outside forces is to strengthen and supplement the local units and not to replace them.

When a riot is on, every hour of communal frenzy adds alarmingly to the piles of dead bodies, burnt houses and properties looted. If this situation is compounded by distrust and lack of rapport between the forces that are called upon to handle the situation and this continues even for a few hours, one can imagine the damage that can be caused to the city. It is therefore necessary to work out in advance the specific units that would be made available for dealing with riots in towns and cities where this problem is of a chronic nature. Their deployment plan can and should be so arranged as to enable them to establish a personal rapport at the subordinate levels. The officers at the subordinate levels are likely to continue in the districts and in the units for much longer spells than the senior officers who get posted out more frequently. This calls for advanced planning and a willingness to accept the fact that the arrangements such as the one suggested are practicable. It is easy to shoot down this suggestion on the ground that it is impractical and visionary. Familiarisation exercises should be carried out periodically with units of the Central Reserve Police Force and a few Border Security Force units, of people and places which are communally very sensitive. An adequate strength of paramilitary units should be stationed in close proximity to these places if not in them. This would facilitate the prompt induction of supplementary units which will not fail to make a qualitative difference in the handling of a communal situation. Considering the stakes involved in terms of bitterness that is generated between the communities, the international implications and the geo-political vested interests of our neighbours in exploiting continued communal disharmony and the damage that it can do to the image of the country as a secular democratic nation, nothing is too much to ensure communal peace. If communal discord cannot be eliminated completely inspite of the best efforts, the least that can be ensured is to make sure that the loss due to such riots is kept down to the very minimum, thereby reducing the propaganda mileage of such tragedies.

VII

Role of the Police

Over a period of time certain elements in the country have developed a vested interest in the frequency and the ferocity of the communal riots. There are several vested interests, and not just one, with different aims and objects. One of these groups uses the occasion to settle scores between criminals belonging to different communities and more so between criminals engaged in illegal but lucrative activities such as smuggling, illicit distillation, bootlegging, gambling and drug pushing. They have a stake in keeping alive the communal virus which they exploit from time to time depending upon the circumstances. This is not to gainsay the fact that the criminals are one class of people whose inter-personal relations normally transcend communal considerations when it comes to their day to day illegal opetrations. They however, do not fail to exploit a situation if their personal or group interests demand it. The killing of Alamzeb on 30th December, 1985 by the Surat Police and the riot that followed in Ahmedabad on the subsequent days is a case in point. Not to proceed against these anti-social elements and allow them to indulge in their activities of organised crime without any serious effort to break into them is a sure invitation to trouble at a place and time of their choosing. Unless therefore, these activities are dealt with sternly and purposefully as an integral and important part of day-to-day public administration, these elements would inevitably become organized syndicates, large and strong enough to be able to purchase political influence and administrative patrongage through their economic power, and to pose a challenge to the powers that be whenever and wherever they may decide to do so. If therefore, the communal riots, in Ahmedabad could continue for several months and the incidence of riots in places like Bhiwandi, Moradabad, Aligarh, Biharsharif and other places is on the increase, it is time that the problem is looked into not merely as a communal problem to be handled as a fire-fighting exercise at the level of the police only. It is to be treated as a socially cancerous disease which has taken root over the years, and towards the growth and sustenance of which several other forces have contributed.

When for politicians, political power at any cost becomes the goal, it is the effectiveness of illegal operations and manipulations which matter and not the time-tested norms and principles. Politicians who rise to power on the strength of such manoeuvrings and manipulations of political operators are for ever hostages to this political culture which has its economic base outside the legal framework and derives sustenance from activities such as sumuggling, bootlegging and the like. A political culture somewhat on these lines had grown over the years in Ahmedabad which had brought about a nexus between the politicians, the police and the anti-socials who are economic and political power brokers.

In 1985 when the reservation agitation began in Ahmedabad, the police force that was called upon to handle the agitation had been corrupted as never before and the image of its leadership at the city level left much to be desired. A senior police officer of the State of Gujarat referred to the syndicates of corruption in the police ranks at the point of the time when the force was called upon to face one of its worst ordeals in the handling of law and order. The officer incharge of the city was under extension and this created its own disciplinary complications in the hierarchy The general belief in the force itself was that the extension of the service of the officer beyond the date of retirement was motivated entirely by political rather than professional considerations and this carried with it its own message down the line which proved detrimental to his effective handling of the crisis that enveloped the city. In cities and towns which are prone to communal riots and where the people have a tendency to take to agitational politics of protest, the choice of functionaries, on whose performance as the leader of the team depend the security of life and property of an entire city, should not be governed by considerations of short-term political advantage and expedience but by the fundamental tenets of administration. Unless and until the choice of the functionaries at all levels of administration, and more so at the fulcrum of power in places which are communally and politically sensitive, are governed by considerations of professional integrity, commitment, competence and leadership, we will continue to invite the type of festering violence that was witnessed in Ahmedabad.

In an unprecedented gesture of unity, the Gujarat Assembly called upon the government to "mercilessly put down communal violence at any cost". The resolution moved by some political party leaders in August, 1985 requested the authorities to be ruthless. One of them said: "In the past we had occasions to complain about the police behaviour. We want to assure the government and the police that we are with you in combating the evil of communalism."

The existence of a nexus between the police, the criminals and the politicians is evident from the Press statement of Julio Riberio(31) who took over as the Chief of the State Police in July 1985. In an interview he is reported to have said: "The police force here has been ruined due to heavy politicisation. Every transfer used to take place at the behest of politicians. Police officers were pressurised to do what politicians wanted. So criminals had a hey-day.... Bootleggers are the main trouble makers. Some of them are gun runners. All this while they have been reigning supreme in the walled city as they had political patronage. Gujarat is a classic example of the nexus that politicians build up with bootleggers. The police are also involved."

Ribeiro has rare qualities of leadership. In addition he was in the happy position of being called upon by the Central government to rescue a city torn by communal conflicts. Having thus come as a deliverer, he could say what he said in the plainest of terms without inviting any reprisal from the powers that be. He might not have spoken out as strongly as he did unless he was convinced that the disease had gone deep into the roots and it was time that someone responsible said that enough was enough. Not being beholden to the local political bosses for the position that he held, he did not have to look over his shoulder for the approval of his actions by the powers-that-be, at the level of the state government. He knew what exactly his task was and from where his mandate came. The Gujarat Police antenna down the line picked up the message fast enough. Men and matters began to fall in the slots meant for each, and the situation fast returned to normal. This carries a very fundamental message and lesson for politicians and administrators generally and for the police in particular.

Without detracting in the slightest from the eminence of Ribeiro who is in a class by himself, it needs to be said that there are officers in the Indian police who are capable of rising to similar heights if only the concerned governments give these officers the same unfettered freedom for non-partisan action in the normal day-to-day administration which the Gujarat government had extended to Ribeiro. It was compelled to do so when conditions had degenerated to a state of near chaos. It is only if and when each Chief of police in the differnet states takes his stand on the day-to-day issues confronting him entirely on their merits, and without fear of political reprisals for professional jobs fearlessly and impartially performed, will we be in a position to eliminate avoidable violence from society. Under these conditions alone could one judge police performance fairly, and hold them accountable if there is excessive and endemic violence. Festering and endemic violence, one may reiterate, is essentially the product of compromises with established norms and standards, be it by the politicians or the police, or worse, by both.

The state of affairs in some of the other states which are plagued by communal conflicts are certainly no better. The point that needs to be made is that if the police, at whatever level and to whatever extent, becomes privy to bootlegging or smuggling or other areas of organized crime, it forfeits its authority to curb anti-social and nefarious activities in the eyes of the people, and thus loses its reason for existence. Instead it becomes a hostage in the hands of these unscrupulous elements who at the slightest sign of the exercise of legitimate authority by guardians of law decide to show the corrupt elements among them their proper place. In the process, the force itself crumbles, depending on the extent to which it is infected When the infection is widespread and down the line, there is very little health and vitality left in the force capable of withstanding effectively the eroding and proliferating problems.

Every compromise in public life with time tested norms and values pushes the threshold of violence further down. Now the moot point is, will the lessons of Gujarat which had been arrived at after such enormous cost in terms of lives, property and defiance of authority, endure at the appropriate levels? If the enlightened awareness belatedly displayed by the legislators of the Gujarat Assembly permeates the motivations and animates the actions of the politicians in the other states, the country will be spared an enormous volume and variety of violence which otherwise may be difficult to avoid.

— —

The riots in Aligarh in August and September, 1979 led to a series of tragic happenings, most of which were because of the lack of rapport between the Senior Superintendent of Police and the officers down the line, though everyone was of the view that the Senior Superintendent of Police(S.S.P.) was personally a man of integrity and courage. The gap in communication between him and his officers contributed to the tragedy more than anything else. Yet no action was taken against those down the line for aggravating the situation by their acts of omission and commission.

Several right-thinking officers of the Bihar Police feel that the rank and file can behave in a communal manner if they are not properly officered and controlled. This is indeed a sad admission. The rank and file in the Police have to bear the brunt in any communal situation. If these people are not capable of even surmounting their caste barriers as should be evident from the fact that in Bihar District Police Lines the Messes are still not only denominational, but even caste based, can they rise above communal considerations?

Both in Moradabad and Aligarh and even in other places there have been allegations of police inaction or even partisanship in dealing with the riots. This is curable if the Armed Police, which is inducted on the occasion of riots is led by responsible officers who are held accountable for the conduct of the men working under them. As long as the men are allowed to function with little or no supervision by responsible officers, such allegations can always be levelled and often not without justification. Every such allegation is an indication of the failure of leadership at the operational level. Making any particular place out of bounds for any particular police unit or removing it from any situation, certainly does not do credit either to the police or to the authorities. Such drastic action against the whole unit is not fair when a large body of men go into action. It is possible that some men may have acted prejudicially and in the process brought the entire force into disrepute. One does come across unscrupulous policemen, who do take advantage of a situation for their own personal aggrandizement. If all such allegations are squarely looked into, and if the small segment of the armed and the district police units responsible for such behaviour are identified, isolated and made examples of, such misconduct on the part of the men is not likely to recur. Instead all such complaints are forgotten once the force is moved out of the scene till they are repeated once again on the next occasion. This is certainly not the manner in which we would ever be able to inculcate the right type of attitude among the security forces in the handling of such delicate situations.

If the successive communal riots in different parts of the country during the last few years have taught us anthing, it is that the Armed Police units employed for handling the riots should be effectively officered by the right type of officers who are known for their general uprightness, straight and impartial dealings. Instead, officers who have been found to be corrupt and devious in their dealings are usually dumped in the Armed Police more as a punishment than as a part of career postings. Such officers when they do come into contact with the agitated crowds in a difficult situation find themselves incapable of leading the men into effective and courageous action. Much less can they control them when the men run berserk out of greed or communal passion or whatever.

The point is where, when and who will go into all such episodes which have relevance to police inaction and partisanship, in all their various implications, draw appropriate lessons and hammer out solutions which can be applied to avoid similar conflicts and misunderstandings in future? A failure to draw objective lessons by the different constituents of the administration has been one of the chronic and continuing defects of the present system, which deals with law and order problems in their several manifestations in different states as incidents away and apart from each other. It may be a simple case of law and order or it may be related to communal problem or student or other problems. The fact remains that the absence of a machinery which would make an ongoing audit and appraisal of the failures, irregularities, and improprieties at different levels and in different units of administration continues to be a serious defect at both the state and the Central level. The same agency could also relay the experiences gained in each difficult situation, as also the notable achievements of individuals or units to the training institutions, which would then incorporate them into the training syllabi. The present adhoc approach to the handling of the problems must be replaced by an institutional approach.

Communal riots which used to be generally an urban phenomenon, have in recent years also infected the rural areas. The Biharsharif riots of April, 1981 had affected the rural areas extensively. Immediate reaction to the communal riot at Bhiwandi in May, 1984 occurred in various villages in Thane district. Many villages coming within the jurisdication of 13 Police Stations in the district were affected. In Thane rural area, 13 persons lost their lives. While it is comparatively easy to handle a riot in the cities and towns where there are facilities available, keeping control of a riotous situation in the rural areas may involve time consuming measures which could also be ineffecitve. In the very nature of it the areas to be tackled will be far more spread out and will have inadequate communication facilities. Police resources in the rural areas as presently provided are extremely poor. By the time any meaningful effort can be organized and put forward, the damage that can occur may well prove to be devastating to the point of becoming a national shame. We have not yet started thinking on these lines. We continue to believe that riots are the exclusive problems of urban areas, and what little thinking has gone into the handling of the problem is by and large limited to the urban centres. The potential for Hindu-Muslim conflicts in the rural areas may be utilised to create violent conflicts by fundamentalists belonging to both the groups. The existing law and order arrangement in the rural areas is woefully inadequate to meet the likely contingencies in most of the states.

Now that the Hindu-Sikh problem has shattered the complacency that we had all along nursed because of the earlier amity between these two communities, it is time that we thought in terms of devising certain radical institutional arrangements in the policing of the rural areas. This will also have to take into account socio-economic changes coming about rapidly in the wake of agrarian reforms, developmental activities and anti-poverty programmes.

Hindu-Sikh harmony has withsood a considerable amount of tension and provocation. The rural areas of the Punjab where the Hindus are in a minority have generally been peaceful, except for the killings of isolated individuals by the extremists. This stands to the credit of the Sikhs who are the majority community in the villages. The same thing however cannot be said about the urban areas of the Punjab where during the first eight months of 1986 clashes had occurred between the Hindus and the Sikhs. What shape this conflict between the two communities in the urban centres of the Punjab will take in times to come, and what effect it will have in the rural areas of the Punjab can only be a matter of speculation.

There are however three distinct strands in the psyche of Sikhs in the Punjab, the impact of which on the Sikh community cannot be minimised. The first is the near-total absence of any worthwhile results by way of criminal prosecution of the anti-socials who were responsible for the senseless killings of the Sikhs and the mindless savagery in the week immediately following the assassination of Mrs. Indira Gandhi. This is a standing grievance nursed by almost the entire Sikh community and more so by the perceptive and the intellectuals among them. The message that has gone around in Punjab in this regard and the impact it would have among the people cannot be minimised. The second strand is the migration of a large number of the relations of the victims of the riots of 1984 from Delhi and other places to Punjab and their settling down there. The Hindus who have either suffered in Punjab or were frightened and have migrated are temporarily sheltered in Delhi and other areas in Himachal and Haryana. They are fresh centres of tension. The wounds of the two communities will continue to be raw for quite sometime to come. In the meantime, to expect that they will not adversely affect the prevailing state of communal amity, is to put a premium on human nature. The third and the most abiding strand which while being very important, and intensely insidious is the Pakistan factor. This has to do with infiltration by Pak elements and the activities of agent-provocateurs who have an abiding interest in the communal discord. Over a period of time, this will not remain merely as a communal problem. This will have to be viewed as an integral part of a long term plan of Pakistan to neutralize that part of her border with India.

Arun Nehru told Parliament in April, 1986 after a visit to Punjab that he had told Barnala, the Chief Minister of Punjab about what was happening in most of the Gurudwaras, which was a matter of serious concern. He had brought to his attention the provocative and anti-national utterances, which the 'Ragis' and 'Dagis' were making in Punjab villages. They were inciting communal passions and creating enormous problems. Some anti-national statements made by some organisations were also brought to his notice. Mr. Nehru spoke of the deepening communal divide. "I spent two days in Punjab and the disturbing feature was that we met many political parties, many groups and individuals and they all talked about the Sikh side or the Hindu side and very few mentioned about the Punjabi side".

In the light of the foregoing, it is very necessary that policing the rural areas of the country receives greater attention than it has so far. This has to be attended to speedily if we are not to be caught unawares.

Ability to prevent a crisis is as integral to the concept of crisis management as managing the crisis itself. Instead of merely helplessly watching developing situations, effective crisis management implies an ability to anticipate and act in a manner commensurate with the nature and dimensions of the problems that are likely to arise in a fast developing society. The manner in which the Police strength of Bhiwandi has increased over the years should explain this point aptly. At the time of the 1970 riots there was only one Police Station with a strength of 192 Policemen which was increased to three after the riots, with a total Police strength of about 469. After the 1984 riots there has been an accretion in the strength of the town Police by about 303. That means the Police strength of the town was substantially increased, evidently as a sequel to the 1984 riots. If only this sudden increase had been graduated over the years to match the proliferating problems of the town, it should have been possible for the administration to keep down the loss of lives and property. The verve, the vigour and vitality of an administration lie in the ability of its institutions to anticipate and act effectively, instead of allowing itself to be overtaken by events.

The problems generated by socio-economic changes and the population incease, with particular reference to the character and composition of this increase make it imperative that the government undertakes at least a decennial review of the Police strength, its deployment and related problems. A more frequent review should be undertaken of the communal problems in the communally prone areas, which should make it possible to spell out the latest steps that the situations demand and which need to be adopted to anticipate conflicts before they arise and to curb and control them effectively and promptly when they do. This periodical review could be a very useful exercise if it is done by a study team consisting of administrators, political leaders, publicmen and police officials. Units of this team can visit the communally sensitive places in an effort to understand and update the assessment of the problems in its several facets. Only such determined and systematic efforts to come to grips with communal problems are likely to yield enduring results.

Conflicts between the followers of different religious is not new in history. There have been wars of religion in the past in several parts of the world. But over a period of time this trend has changed and the conflict has shifted from religion to other forms. In this connection the observations of Arthur Koestler would be relevant(32) : "It is not a novelty in history that a real dilemma which once seemed all important is gradually drained of its meaning and becomes pseudo-dilemma as new historical realities emerge. People lost interest in waging wars of religion when national consciousness began to dawn on them. Every period seems to have its specific conflict which polarises the world and serves as an ideological compass in the chaos, until history passes over it with a shrug, and afterwards people wonder what they were so excited about. It is a further fact that some of these great ideological conflicts are never decided; They end in a stalemate. Instead of a decision there came a deadlock and a process which one might call the withering away of the deadlock. The withering or draining of meaning always seems to be the result of some mutation in human consciousness accompanied by a shift of emphasis to an entirely different set of values, from religious consciousness to national consciousness, to economic consciousness and so on." One hopes that the history of our times will similarly tide over the present unhappy phase leaving the people wondering about the senselessness of communal conflicts. To expect however that his would happen without any deliberate effort on the part of the government and the people is to abdicate the role and responsibility that history enjoins on the present generation of people and politicians.

VIII

Imperatives of Secularism

Secularism is a concept of political philosophy and constitutional doctrine. True, it is not a moral concept, but nor is it something to be tampered with or circumvented by one device or another to suit political expediency. It has to be accepted unreservedly as a basic principle to regulate the actions of the state at all levels in a nation comprising of people of different religious faiths.

The provisions with regard to secularism which have been embodied under the Fundamental rights, and which figure in Articles 25, 26, 27, 28, 29 and 30 of the Indian Constitution are not the outcome of a people's movement launched with a specific purpose in view. It was in fact the product of a set of historical forces and political developments which had culminated in the tragedy of the partition of the country and the trail of human misery following the brutal killings of thousands of people belonging to different communities in both parts of the divided country. Since the very idea of partition was conceived and consummated in the context of a communal ideology, the Founding Fathers of the Indian Constitution wanted to ensure from the very beginning that in the India of their hopes and dreams politics should never again figure as an integral programme of the communal organisations of the country. This explains their motivation as also their anxiety in the resolution that the Constituent Assembly passed on the 3rd April, 1948. The resolution runs as follows :

"Whereas it is essential for the proper functioning of democracy and the growth of national unity and solidarity that communalism should be eliminated from Indian life, this Assembly is of the opinion that no communal organisation which by its constitution or by the exercise of discretionary power vested in any of its officers or organizers admits to or excludes from its membership persons on grounds of religion, race, caste or any of them, should be permitted to engage in any activities other than those essential for the bonafide religious, cultural, social and educational needs of the community, and that all steps, legislative and administrative necessary to prevent such activities should be taken."

The resolution is eloquent not so much in what it includes as what in effect it excludes. According to the resolution, among the several activities which are open to communal organisations, politics is conspicuous by its absence. Yet, can it be said in the light of all that has been happening in the country during the last three decades, that the communal organisations of the country have been limiting their activities to the letter and spirit of the above resolution? The importance that the first Prime Minister of the country, Pandit Jawaharlal Nehru, attached to the resolution passed by the Constituent Assembly should be clear from the letter which he wrote to the Chief Ministers of States (then Provinces) on 3rd May, 1948. The letter ran as follows:

"We have noticed a recrudescence of communal movements. The old R.S.S. is raising its head again in various forms and all kinds of rumours are afloat. I trust that your province will not permit this development. I would also like to draw your special attention to the resolution in regard to communal organisations passed by the Constituent Assembly. WE HAVE STATED THAT WE WILL NOT RECOGNIZE OR ENCOURAGE IN ANY WAY ANY COMMUNAL ORGANISATION WHICH HAS POLITICAL ENDS. I HOPE THAT YOUR GOVERNMENT WILL ALSO FOLLOW THIS POLICY" (Emphasis supplied). Contrary to all such exhortations, several blatantly communal organisations are functioning today with avowed political objectives. We as a nation have been travelling in a direction totally opposite to the one that was set out for us by the Founding Fathers.

Article 25 of the Constitution while providing for freedom of conscience and the right to freely profess, practice and propagate religion also ensures through Article 25(2) that nothing in this Article shall affect the operation of any existing law or prevent the state from making any law – regulating or restricting any economic, financial, *political or other secular activities* (emphasis supplied) which may be associated with religious practice.

Secularism implies two imperatives : First, a secular state ensures that each of its citizen enjoys complete freedom of religion in so far as it relates to the relationship that each individual wants to arrive at between himself and his Maker or wishes to pursue as his moral or spiritual goal. If community prayers and community observance of religion are conducted subject to public order, and other restrictions enumerated in Article 25(1) or Article 26 of the Constitution, there should be no cause for conflict. Article 26 reads as follows :

"Subject to public order, morality and health, every religious denomination or any section thereof shall have the right :

(a) to establish and maintain institutions for religious and charitable purposes;
(b) to manage its own affairs in matters of religion;
(c) to own and acquire moveable and immoveable property; and
(d) to administer such property in accordance with law.

The second imperative is that the citizen either in his individual capacity or in his group activities with regard to religion does not intrude into the affairs of the state, thereby enabling the state to carry on its functions in conditions characterised by freedom from religion. Thus secularisation as a concept of state policy will be real and meaningful only in an atmosphere which guarantees both freedom of religion and freedom from religion. It is as important for the state to enjoy the status of freedom from regilion in its political activities as it is for the citizens to have freedom of religion. It is only when these two propositions which are in one sense, mutually exclusive, co-exist and are accepted together that secularism will come alive. Only as and when, we, the people of India, are able to elevate secularism to this level as a practical doctrine, would we be able to vindicate the hopes of our Founding Fathers as enshrined in the Constituent Assembly resolution of 1948 and the relevant provisions of the Constitution.

The measure of anxiety that the architects of our Constitution had with regard to ensuring the welfare of the minority communities is more than amply reflected in the protection that they extended to the cultural and educational rights of the minority communities through Article 29 and 30 of the Constitution. At the same time the state kept itself away from the charge of promoting religious instructions of whatever denomination by stipulating in Article 28(1) that:

"No religious instructions shall be provided in any educational institution wholly maintained out of state funds." Article 28(3) of the Constitution stipulates that: "No person attending any educational institution recognised by the state or receiving aid out of state funds shall be required to take part in any religious instructions that may be imparted in such institutions or to attend any religious worship that may be conducted in such institutions or in any premises attached thereto unless such person or, if such person is a minor, his guardian has given his consent thereto."

In the light of the Constitutional provisions cited above there should be no doubt about the rsponsibility of the state to ensure that the government of the country is conducted on secular lines. Apart from the specific provisions in the Articles from 25 to 30 of the Constitution, secularism did not figure as such in the Preamble of the Constitution. Even this gap, if indeed it was a gap, was sought to be filled by the 42nd Amendment of the Constitution in 1976, when the term 'socialist secular' was added to the Preamble of our Constitution, which in its amended from read as 'sovereign socialist secular democratic republic'. It needs to be made clear that the 42nd Amendment did not introduce any new concept on the subject of secularism which had not been already provided for in the Articles of the Constitution. It only made the concept explicit and brought it to the notice of the general public by incorporating it in the Preamble of the Constitution.

In a country like India with its diversities, and particularly, multiplicity of religions, secularism to be meaningful has to have in its believers and practitioners a mental infrastructure and attitude which with genuine tolcrance of each other's religion is also capable of generating mutual goodwill among the people of different faiths and religions. This calls for an understanding at all levels of the essence which is the same in all religions, as distinct from the externals and rituals which differ from religions to religion. Fundamentally, religious beliefs may not lend themselves to being proved by reasoning or logic. What endows religion with all that is grand is exactly its non-amenability to logical proof. Martin Luther King went to the length of saying that : "reason is the greatest enemy that faith has". For the general mass of people a God that is accessible would rob them of the mystique and wonderment which is what religion is all about. This does not imply that religion in any form and for whatever reason needs to encroach on the affairs of the state.

Secularism to become a fact of life has to be lived through by the people as a whole and not merely preached from the political platforms by a few. This has to be, so to say, an article of faith, and not a strategy. The chances of its acceptance and being acted upon by the vast mass of the people will largely depend on the consistent efforts and initiatives taken on several fronts by the state, and voluntary organisations to make it a fighting faith, integral to the culture and ethos of the country. That being the goal to be pursued, to expect that it will be realised just by virtue of the place that it finds in the Preamble and the Articles of our Constitution, and thus play a self-fulfilling role in the life of the nation, is to substitute pious hopes for resolute and persistent political action. The least that we can do to start with is not to accentuate the communal divide by feulling it on grounds of political and administrative expediency. In this context, the observation of Gandhiji is relevant. He said : "There are as many religions as there are individuals; but those who are conscious of the spirit of nationality do not interfere with one another's religion. If Hindus believe that India should be peopled only by Hindus, they are living in a dream land. The Hindus, the Sikhs, the Mohammadens, the Parsis and the Christians who have made India their country, are fellow countrymen and they will have to live in unity if only for their interest. In no part of the world are one nationality and one religion synonymous terms; nor has it ever been so in India."

Secularism is not compatible with denominational political parties. When a denominational political party fights an election it appeals to communalism and not secularism for its vote. We as a nation do not seem to realise that we are also the victims of our own double-think. We want the prestige and pleasures of a secular state without going through the pains and hazards of doing away with blatantly communal parties. The dichotomy of our public life consists exactly in this. When religion becomes, directly or indirectly, a function of community consolidation for political purposes it does so at the cost of national integration. In such an environment, the votaries of the community's religion become the architects of the communal divide.

There is no intention to minimise the difficulties that we have to go through in the process of living up to the demands of a secular state. A beginning has to be made somewhere if this objective, which remains enshrined in our Constitution, is not to languish indefinitely. To expect that the people will usher in secularism without the state itself discharging its share of the responsibility is to indulge in illusions. Let the political parties get started even by de-communalising their day-to-day activities and with it the activities and calculations related to elections. It could well turn out to be the most significant first step, and a fruitful approach to a seemingly intimidating job.

IX

Islands of Hope

While discussing the communal problem we should also remember that there are mixed localities in Surat, Varanasi, Aligarh and other places where the communities have retained their sanity and have not allowed themselves to become victims of communal frenzy. On the country, there is so much of mutual business dependence between them that they have developed almost a vested interest in peace.

Notwithstanding the arousal of intense communal passions, there were many instances in all the riots, of Hindus and Muslims working together to keep their localities free from attacks by mobs from other localities and thus maintaining communal harmony.

In Surat, a large number of Muslims employ Hindu migrant labour from Uttar Pradesh, Bihar and Andhra Pradesh. The Hindus too employ Muslim migrants from these places. How is it that they have been able to achieve a degree of emotional and communal amity when the same thing is missing in other places ? Evidently, the factors which cause riots in other places have been absent in Surat. As the Police Commissioner of Surat put it, Surat has not had a communal riot for several decades even though this is a city which has a sizeable minority population (15.65%) and a very flourishing business centre where members belonging to the minority community are employed in large numbers by the majority community employers and vice versa. As the Collector at Varanasi put it : "The relationship between the two communities is one of Tana-Bana (warp and weft). Another officer who had worked as Collector at Aligarh explained how even during the worst periods of tension, in areas where lock manufacturing goes on in houses, the sales tax collection from the areas did not register any decline except for very brief periods, which showed that the relations and trade between the communities continued without any serious interruption even though certain other parts of the state were plagued by riots.

Some of the eminent scholars such as Rashiddudin Khan, Imtiaz Ahmed, Moin Shakir among others are all agreed that the Muslims as a community are as much fragmented as the Hindus because of class, caste and linguistic cleavages. That being the inherent nature of the Muslim community, the chances of their identifying themselves with the class interests in the rest of the country would have been far greater had it not been for the community leaders among them exploiting for their personal purposes the perceived or the actual-grievances of the community. What is basically an act of exploitation assumes legitimacy and respectability when it is pitted against the equally communal forces among the Hindus. Incidents like those caused by throwing open the disputed place in Ayodhya for worship by Hindus, will only provide the required proof that the Muslims are being discriminated against. We just cannot unscramble history. Such agitations will only make the communal divide more and more rigid, making co-existence between the communities difficult over the years.

Hindus as the majority community have a responsibility to ensure that they do not take the lead in provoking the minorities. Unfortunately however, the past record of the majority community has not fulfilled this hope. It is only when the majority community displays restraint and forbearance even in circumstances of extreme provocation that we would be anywhere near communal amity. It is generally believed that Hinduism is not so much a religion as a way of life. The essence of it lies in its ability to live and let live. Tolerance is its basic tenet. Judged by this standard, can it be said that in general the present practitioners of the ancient religion are true to the faith ? That there should have been a protest and a demonstration even against an innocuous and yet a historic occasion such as the visit of the Pope to this country in 1986, is a measure of the intolerance, however, microscopic and insignificant this demonstration was compared to the vast mass of the Hindu population who happily welcomed the visit. It needs to be made clear that communalism among the minorities can very often be the by-product of a sense of insecurity vis-a-vis the majority community. This can adequately be dealt with given the institutional infrastructure. Communalism of the majority community can be far more destructive and devastating of all the values that India has stood for and preserved over the centuries. In short, it will cease to be the cultural entity epitomising within its fold the values of the several phases of Indian civilization to which it has been the legitimate and proud heir and become in effect a mere geographical expression and entity. Tolerance is to be tested against provocation just as resistence is to be tested against temptation. If there is nothing to provoke, where is the scope for the display or measure of tolerance? The plural society like the one in the prevailing conditions in India is something of a melting pot of several religious groups, social and economic interests and cultures.

If the slogan 'Unity in diversity' is to be at all meaningful, it involves the evolution of a value system, in which tolerance has to be an important component. A plural society can become a functioning and self fulfilling reality only when the majority conducts itself even under the most difficult and provocative conditions in a manner that it does not alienate or antagonise the minorities.

The process of integration implies a degree of give and take between different cultures which is what the Indian ethos is all about. Any resistance to this will inevitably invlove a measure of conflict between the communities for which no one community can be held solely responsible. The minority communities will understandably have their own fears of being swamped by the majority community. The majority community has the responsibility to ensure that it does not tyrannise over the minorities. But each community has to contribute towards building a secular country, if necessary by surrendering a part of its identity in the interests of the whole. This is, after all, not so very different from the running of a joint family, where while each one surrenders something of his or her interests and preferences for the harmonious well being of the whole, still retains his or her own personal identity. The ease and willingness with which each community plays the role that is expected of it in the context of its religious identity and culture will decide whether or not there will be conflicts between the communities and consequent violence or cohesion and harmony.

The backward class of Muslims or Momins mainly composed of craftsman, artisans, weavers and other similar groups, have come by a new affluence consequent on the expansion of the handicrafts industry. According to Imtiaz Ahmed, the wealthy butchers in North India have opened cold storages, rice and flour mills and hotels. The socio-economic changes that have been a dominant feature of post-Independent India have benefitted the Muslims as much as the others. This neo-elite group is a new force in the Muslim politics in the north, particularly in Uttar Pradesh and Bihar. Mohammed Aslam (33) in his article 'Muslim identity and Politics', had pointed out that the Muslim convention held at Lucknow in 1980 had broken up as the neo-elites were more interested in projecting their economic demands than demands relating to their personal law, Urdu and similar issues. "In a sense, it can be argued that the politicisation of the backward class of Muslims has brought greater fragmentation in the Muslim population as well as greater secularisation, which is indeed a very positive and healthy development. But it must be remembered that whenever the interests of these classes are threatened by the eruption of communal violence they are forced to join hands with communal politics and the forces of Islamic resurgence."

The inter-dependence between the Hindus and the Muslims in trade and commerce in places like Varanasi, Moradabad, Aligarh and other places have given rise to pressure groups among the artisans and weavers who put pressure on the fanatical members of their respective communities to call off the projection of any communal issue as in the process the communities stand to lose economically. This has created for once a vested interest in peace between the communities. It is important that in times of peace a proper survey and study of these areas should be made with a view to understanding and evaluating the cultural, economic and political implications of the trade relationship that is being built up between the communities on an almost day-to-day basis, without either of the groups being consciously aware of the fact that in their working together to promote the joint economic interests of both the groups, they are also contributing to the secularisation of the Indian socio-economic and political system.

These may become the bastions of our secularism. They have come into being not because of any conscious effort by the state or by any political party, but often inspite of them. They are the product of the basic good sense of the people, living and growing together against common odds that are the inevitable concomitants of the economic struggle for existence in conditions of scarce resources and limited opportunities. It is when such conditions, which are about the same for all sections of the people, are exploited by the communal elements for promoting their vested interests that these people whose exacting mechanics of life leave them no time beyond earning their daily pittance, become parties to, and eventually the victims of, communal violence. Left to themselves, they can rise, and have risen, above the religious divide. These are our islands of hope, of sustenance, and of the eventual survival of secularism as it was conceived by the Founding Fathers. No effort is too great to make these islands expand and embrace the whole country, reclaiming in the process those areas which are temporarily stranded in the communal backwaters.

In the type of situation that is developing in our country, it is difficult to think in terms of a grand strategy which can purge the communities of the misunderstandings and suspicions that they have against each other. Considering the general selfishness and evil in human nature, one cannot dream on the lines of a visionary and plan an utopia. What can be attempted and which is worth working for is to restrain and curb the violence that is inherent in all such conflicts as and when they arise. A modest approach on these lines is, I think, capable of yielding results which over a period of time should have an impact on the incidence and the intensity of communal violence.

Education is one field where a lot can be done to promote communal understanding and amity, at an age when if it takes root it will endure. The Minority Commission in its Fourth Annual Report also laid special stress on 'synthesising patterns of thoughts and feelings which would stem the tide of disintegrating forces'. Can we think in terms of having common schools for all communities instead of having denominational schools exclusively for the children of one community? Mixed educational institutions where a cross section of students drawn from all communities study and play together would certainly promote and contribute to national integration. Above all it is necessary to ensure and improve the secular nature and content of text books that are prescribed in schools and colleges. There have been complaints in this regard. There have been allegations about uncomplimentary references made to the Muslim rulers of India in history text books taught to students. Special care is essential in the preparation of text books, the contents of which will eventually influence the attitudes of the youth to each other's community.

If the number of Madrassas that have grown over the years in Bihar, West Bengal and Uttar Pradesh is any guide, it is indicative of the fact that some sections of the Muslim community would like to have its children put through the primary stages exclusively in the Madrassas. Since many of these children do not pursue their studies at higher levels because of economic reasons, the only education that they would have the benefit of is what would be imparted to them from the religious angle. Thus they would not have the benefit of general education and this would have its own disadvantage and will distort their outlook. In view of the continued backwardness of the vast mass of Muslims in the field of education, it seems imperative that special steps are taken by the state to increase and improve the facilities and opportunities for their formal and vocational education, which may supplement their religious education.

Inaugurating the Conference on National Integration on September 28 1961, Dr. S. Radhakrishnan, the then Vice President of India, observed : "National integration cannot be built by brick and mortar; it cannot be built by chisel and hammer. It has to grow silently in the minds and hearts of men. The only process is the process of education. That may be a slow process but it is a steady thing. It is a permanent thing. It is the one thing by which we will be able to transform our people".

Enough data have been provided to enable us to conclude that the percentage of Muslims going in for higher levels of education is far lower than what is warranted by the strength of their population. It is obviously necessary that this percentage improves if the Muslim representation in the tertiary sector is to match their population percentage. This would be possible only if the large bulk of the weaker sections among the Muslims do not become drop outs after the primary stage, or if these sections avail of general education and not restrict themselves to Madrassas. More schools should be set up in areas peopled by the weaker sections among the Muslims and other communities. Let religious education be a supplement to the general education by all means, but not a substitute if the Muslims are to take their rightful place in the tertiary sector of the economy of the country.

Television as a mass media can be fully exploited to highlight such aspects of life between the communities which unite us as Indians rather than divide us as religious communities. This would mean harnessing the services of intellectuals and literateurs who can produce plays and films with an accent on communal harmony. The impact that Television has is far more powerful and enduring than any other means of conveying the message of communal harmony.

Another area in which bridges can be built between the communities is through joint celebrations of festivals as in the case of 'Onam' in Kerala, in which members of all communities participate. Public celebrations of religious festivals through processions and pageants can be reduced, and to that extent communal clashes and conflicts can also be reduced. But wherever celebrations do take place, a conscious effort to enlist the cooperation and participation of the other communities should reduce the chances of conflict. It is not unusual for Muslims to participate in Dussehra celebrations or for Hindus to participate in the festivities of Id. Let a determined effort be initiated towards such moves, which will surely blunt the cutting edge of communalism.

Land grabbing in the name of religion for shrines, graves and places of worship has now become sadly frequent. This brings in its wake considerable illwill and tension between communities. Religion, instead of being a bridge of understanding and goodwill between the communities, has become a source of death and destrunction. Today in India the followers of different religions preach not so much the religious beliefs of their saints and seers, but appeal to religious and communal passions. No wonder that the worst crimes against humanity are being committed in the name of religion. This has never been demonstrated more savagely in Independent India than in the recent years.

Whatever may have been the justification for the manner in which the religious festivals were celebrated in the past, the constraints of modern living and the plural society that we live in do not permit the pomp and the papeantry that traditionally characterised the celebrations and festivities. Many old places of worship are now in crowded areas inhabited by different communities. The thoroughfares are choked with people, and the streets do not permit of easy movement even for individuals let alone for large religious processions in their traditional forms. These processions have the potential for disturbing the peace between the communities as has been demonstrated again and again. That such processions are on the increase generally all over the country should be evident from the trend, about which there is authentic information with regard to at least one important state. The Minister of State for Home of the Maharashtra government stated in answer to an Assembly question in the Maharashtra Vidhan Sabha on 11th July 1986 that as many as 68 Rath Yatras had been taken out in the first half of 1986 as against 4 in 1985; 513 Ambedkar Anniversary processions against 13 in the previous year and 944 Shivaji Jayanti processions compared to 656 in 1985. The July 1986 communal riots in Ahmedabad arising again out of a procession illustrates how the authorities can fail to prevent a communal riot even though they have adequate advance warning and knowledge about the possible consequences of such an event. This is so when a procession is taken out more as a demonstration of the strength of a particular community than as a mark of religious devotion. It would be saner, safer, and more decent and dignified to limit all such celebrations to open places where people of the same faith and such others drawn from other communities as would like to participate, can congregate and celebrate the rituals and the festivities. This can be so much more peaceful and satisfying than taking riotous processions through streets and lanes, infuriating in the process people who perceive these processions more as a nuisance than anything sacred. The types of processions that have become common among most of the communities are fast degenerating into competing revivalism, encouraged by governments proclaiming holidays on the slightest excuse. There has to be a policy decision arrived at in consultation with the religious leaders of the different communities with regard to these festivities, processions and celebrations. One cannot vouch for the success of such an effort initially. Since however no conscious and deliberate effort has been made so far on this account at a sufficiently high level at the Centre and in the states, nor by religious leaders who command respect at the national level, this exercise is worth attempting.

Whether or not the communities and the government can arrive at a proper decision acceptable to all with regard to these processions., there is certainly a case for a national policy decision on the screening of these processions on the television. It is worth inquiring whether the coverage of these processions by television contributes towards swelling the crowds who participate in them or heightening their fervour.

Considering the type of fall-out from the conflict arising out of the dispute regarding the reopening of the temple/mosque in Ayodhya, a policy decision appears necessary at the all-India level to put an embargo on the reopening of issues involving old temples and mosques, and shrines of saints. There are several such areas of dispute in Uttar Pradesh, Maharashtra and other places. Unless these issues are treated as finally closed and are not permitted to be reopened on any account, they can well provide the little needed grist to the communal mill.

Most riots take place in the old city centres, which were once upon a time the hub of economic, commercial, and even political and cultural activities. Over the centuries these have grown into veritable slums with very inadequate civic amenities, resulting in appalling living conditions. The narrow lanes and by-lanes do not permit of the volume and variety of modern vehicular traffic. In times of trouble police mobility is thwarted by road blocks and missiles flying from roof tops, and sniping by rioters. Modern town planners have virtually by-passed these centres. These are the areas with mixed population. In short, they are the ghettos and are the tinder boxes which can be ignited by the slightest generation of heat arising out of the flimsiest of causes. They are the haunts of the unemployed, the smugglers, drug peddlers, prostitutes, crime syndicates, liquor dons and the like. They are relatively 'unadministered'. The riots are mostly confined to these areas and seldom spread to the comparatively recent and modern residential areas. It speaks for the virulence that the commuanl poison has acquired over the years that even some other residential area are beginning to get affected by it. If therefore we are to make a dent on the communal front, this will have a lot to do with the town planning exercise, city improvement, decongestation of selected areas, moving out noxious trades and a planned programme of civic housing. If the old city centres are not to explode recurrently they will have to be attended to and rejuvenated. The municipalities and the corporations should collect and deploy more funds on development of civic amenities, education, social welfare activities and programmes to improve the health and hygiene of the places.

Cooperative organisation with mixed membership as has been tried by the Vishwa Bharti Spinning Mills in Bhiwandi would be a good and innovative effort to bring the communities together. Such cooperative efforts should extend also to housing and other programmes undertaken by the developmental authorities.

There are several national activities which can and are contributing to the secularisation and the integration of the country. The three Armed Forces of the country are some of the most important institutions which stand as an abiding testimony to our secular ideals and that of the integrity of the country. Officers from all communities in the three Services have done our country proud both in peace and war. The National Roll of Honour of War Heroes has the names of martyrs drawn from all communities who braved death so that the India of their hopes and dreams may live. We will prove ourselves unworthy of their supreme sacrifice by doing or failing to do anything which would in any way contribute to the cancer of communalism. A little known fact, but nonetheless of very vital significance, is the composition of the officers at the Headquarters in the three Services. They are drawn from different communities and each in his sensitive post is engaged in jobs which are crucial to the security of the country. Each one performs the role allotted to him on the basis of mutual faith and confidence. These are indeed very heartwarming daily experiences of the secularisation and the integrity of the country.

Art an culture are yet another area which has contributed considerably to promoting national integration and secularisation of the country. The technological progress that the country has achieved has largely been the result of the people belonging to different faiths and communities coming together, each contributing significantly to the several achievements that stand to the credit of the nation. The extensive social inter-dependence, trade and communication are some of the other factors which over a period of time should bring about further secularisation of communities and in the process provide additional bonds of national integration. It will be a worthwhile exercise to extend and enlarge these several areas where communal amity and goodwill have contributed significantly to the results achieved by the several teams.

The institution of Home Guards, unfortunately, has not been put to its optimal use. Considering the proliferation of areas which are communally very sensitive, it is not possible to effectively stretch the existing strength of the police to cover all the communal areas unless a complete reorganisation of the police system is attempted and the police strength suitably increased. Even after raising it to the point permitted by the financial constraints, we would not be in a position to say that we have adequate police strength to contain and control the communal problems. It is a pity that we are not putting to maximum use some excellent human material which is available in the form of Home Guards at all places and which to an extent is also organized. If however some more inputs in terms of organisation, training and worthwhile monetary incentives are provided we should have at each of the communally sensitive places a considerable section of local population with full knowledge of people and problems who can be mobilized at short notice for a spell of disciplined and dedicated service. This wing of the Home Guards will have to be brought into being in the context of the changing social scene in India. They may be designated as Citizen Guards and kept as a wing of the Home Guards, if necessary, but used exclusively for dealing with communal riots in coordination with the Peace Committees which spring up on such occasions. The Citizen Guards could well be the cutting edge of the Peace Committee working in close cooperation with the local police These forces could be mobilized not only on occasions of communal tension but also for dealing with caste conflicts as and when it should emerge in some of the states. The institution of Citizen Guards coupled with the institution of Honorary Magistrates should be an effective infrastructural additon to deal with fast changing and developing situations. These two institutions should be kept in a state of preparedness at short notice in all communally prone areas. Since they will have a good mix of the local population, this will take care of the communal composition of the men and officers who are pressed into service in any of the local places. In peace time when they are not used, they should be suitably oriented by lectures and part-time training programmes on the social needs of the area where they may be called upon to lend their services.

Handling the visiting foreign nationals of Pakistan and Bangladesh exclusively at the State level only has serious operational limitations. This is one of those subjects, the coordination of which between the States should be the responsibility of a central agency. Considering the number of Pakistanis and Bangladeshis who visit the country on valid documents it would be difficult for any state agency by itself to keep track of all of them and their inter-State movements and ensure their eventual return to their home land. But these difficulties may be comparatively less if this problem is coordinated at the level of the Central government. The arrangement suggested would enable a better and a more purposeful monitoring of the intentions and activities of the visitors from Pakistan and Bangladesh than it has been possible for us to do through the present arrangement.

There had been occasions when even the best political leadership at the State government level had not been able to avert a communal riot. What a strong, well meaning and effective leadership can do is to get on top of a violent situation promptly and keep down to the minimum the loss of lives and damage to property. Considering the compulsions of communal conflict, the least that the ruling political parties can do is to ensure that the choice of leadership at the state level of the party in power is made only after taking into account the character, competence and the intrinsic worth of the individual in measuring up to the challenges that the affairs of the state generally and the communal problems in particular would expose him to. But when adhocism and political expediency get priority over factors which should be fundamental to the choice of a leader, the state gets inevitably saddled with a political leadership which is weak, ineffective and indecisive. To expect that such a leadership would be able in an emergency to steer the ship of state through the shoals of communal and agitational violence is to substitute hope for reality. The dynamics of current day events are such that by the time the Central leadership comes to the rescue and reinforcement of the timid and vacillating or otherwise seriously flawed state leadership, the damage done to life and property could well be vast and irretrievable. In states, therefore, which are prone to communal violence, the political leader chosen to preside over the destiny of the state government must be capable of riding firmly and fearlessly over violence in public life generally, and communal violence in particular. This is an imperative which those concerned can ill afford to ignore.

While handling communalism what seems immediately an easy path may well well prove ultimately to be the most dangerous one. Expediency as a policy has never succeeded in the long run. This has a special and compelling relevance when dealing with communalism. The long-term and enduring interest of the country consists in doing immediately what the state would have to do ultimately, if the people are to be spared the fatal result of slow haemorrhaging. As of now, it would not be far wrong if the present generation of Indians get the unique distinction of being described by the historians of this era as a band of people who sought to establish a secular state without the people themselves practising secularism. It is the capability and actual performance and not the stated intentions to be a secular state, that will ultimately matter. Not to try and take the initial first step while we do have the capacity and intention to try would be unworthy of our generation. This is one of those Gordian knots which would become increasingly difficult to cut with every passing year. It would be a sad omission which our children will not fail to hold against us. The decision that is waiting to be made will affect not only our own destinies but the future generations, born and unborn.

One would be naive to conclude that communalism over the years has been a diminishing phenomenon. On the contrary, the evil appears to have taken a far more vicious grip on certain sections of the people. This is a very disturbing trend. If the communal groups do not desist from mutually fuelling each other's communalism on the lines that have been witnessed in the recent past, the country will be set on the high road to communal conflicts, the dimension and diabolism of which wil make the past riots seem like trivial incidents. One survives so much that one mistakenly thinks one can survive anthing. But this is not so much a cry of despair as a note of warning. The monster of communalism can be faced and faced squarely when the values of our national life, as envisioned and epitomised in the Preamble of our Constitution, are reflected fully and uniformly in all spheres of our public life, including in particular in state politics and legislations. This is an imperative which cannot be shirked or shrugged off. What is at stake is the integrity of the country. To interpret every warning of disaster and tragedy as a prophecy of doom is as absurd and irrational as treating every soothsayer as the purveyor of truth.

Bibliography

1) Gopal Krishna: 'Communal violence in India', Economic and Political Weekly, Dt. 12th January, 1985.
2) 'Communal violence and its impact on development and national integration, Maharashtra (Bhiwandi and Pune), August, 1985' The Centre for Rural Research and Industrial Development, Chandigarh.
3) D.R. Goyal: 'Ayodhya and After', Mainstream, Dt. 13th March, 1986.
4) Gulam Nabi Khayal: 'Unrest in the Valley', The Illustrated Weekly of India, Dt. 20th October, 1985.
5) Indian Express, Dt. 25th April, 1986.
6) The Hindu, Dt. 17th March, 1986.
7) The Hindu, Dt. 30th July, 1986.
8) Indian Express, Dt. 2nd April, 1986.
9) Ashish K. Biswas: 'The silent tide of human invasion', The Hindu, Dt. 4th April, 1986.
10) Daniel Latif: 'Pak Divorce Law Shames India', The Times of India, Dt. 5th May, 1986.
11. M.R.A. Baig, 'The Muslim Dilemma in India' (1974).
12) M.C. Chagla, 'Roses in December', an autobiography (1973).
13) Tahir Mohammad: 'Personal Law'. This article in Seminar August, 1979 is from the author's book: 'Muslim Personal Law, Role of the State in the Subcontinent'.
14) Mohabubul Hok's article in Quest, September-October, 1971. Quoted by M.R.A. Baig in his book: 'Muslim Dilemma in India' 1974.
15) Ahmed Rashid Sherwani: 'Educational Backwardness', Seminar, August, 1979.
16) A.R. Sayed of Jamia Milia Islamia: 'Orthodoxy', Seminar, August, 1979.

17) Syed Shahbuddin: 'The Indian Muslim in search of his future', The Illustrated Weekly of India, Ist April, 1981.
18) N.C. Saxena: 'Public Employment and Educational Backwardness among Muslims in India', Political Science Review, April-September, 1983.
19) S. Naseem A. Zaidi: 'Employment of Muslims in Public Services: A case study of Aligarh Muslim University', August, 1983. Quoted by N.C. Saxena.
20) IBID N.C. Saxena's article.
21) Naseem A. Zaidi: 'Muslims in Public Services: No bias', The Times of India, Dt. 8th May, 1986.
22) IBID N.C. Saxena's article.
23) Ashgar Ali Engineer: 'Indian Muslims—A study of the Minority Problem in India' (1986).
24) Dr. Zakir Hussain's speech at the Conference on National Integration in 1961.
25) Ashgar Ali Engineer, Economic and Political Weekly, Dt. 15th August, 1981.
26) Mainstream, Dt. 4th May, 1981.
27) Jagmohan Reddy Commission which inquired into the Ahmedabd riots of 1969.
28) The Madon Commission which inquired into the Bhiwandi riots of 1970.
29) Justice Raghubir Dayal Commission which inquired into the Ranchi-Hatia riots 1967
30) Justice Jitendra Narayan Commission which inquired into the Jamshedpur riots of 1979.
31) India Today, August 15, 1985.
32) Arthur Koestler, 'An outgrown dilemma' (1950) in his book: 'In the trail of the Dinasaur' (1955).
33) Mohammad Aslam: 'Muslim Identity and Politics', in his book: Multi Ethnicity and National Integration (1985).